Letters to Talia

Letters to Talia

Dov Indig

Translated from the Hebrew by **Yehuda Burdman**

gefen
publishing house
JERUSALEM • NEW YORK
Est. 1981

EDITOR OF THE HEBREW EDITION: Hagi Ben-Artzi
COVER DESIGN: Tamar Bar Dayan
TYPESETTING: Benjie Herskowitz, Etc. Studios

ISBN: 978-965-229-601-6

3 5 7 9 8 6 4

Gefen Publishing House Ltd.
6 Hatzvi Street
Jerusalem 94386, Israel
972-2-538-0247
orders@gefenpublishing.com

Gefen Books
11 Edison Place
Springfield, NJ 07081
516-593-1234
orders@gefenpublishing.com

www.gefenpublishing.com

Printed in Israel

Send for our free catalogue

Library of Congress Cataloging-in-Publication Data

Indig, Dov, 1951–1973.
[Mikhtavim le-Taliah. English]
Letters to Talia / Dov Indig; Hebrew edition compiled by
Hagi Ben-Artzi; translated from the Hebrew by Yehuda Burdman.
p. cm.
ISBN 978-965-229-601-6
1. Indig, Dov, 1951–1973—Correspondence.
2. Talyah—Correspondence. 3. Israel. Tseva haganah
le-Yisra'el—Officers—Correspondence.
I. Ben-Artzi, Hagi. II. Title.
CT1919.P38I53513 2012
956.9405'40922—dc23
                              2012031093

To the blessed memory of

Dov's sister-in-law

Nava Indig, *z"l*

June 17, 1958 – March 27, 2012

whose life personified

generosity and kindness

CONTENTS

Dov Indig, *z"l*, 1951–1973

FOREWORD

Dov Indig was killed on October 7, 1973, in a holding action on the Golan Heights during the Yom Kippur War. In a book published in his memory by family and friends, excerpts were quoted from an extensive correspondence Dov maintained with Talia,[1] a girl from a secular kibbutz in northern Israel at the beginning of the 1970s. At the time, Talia was a high school student, and Dov was a student in the *hesder* yeshiva Kerem B'Yavneh, near Ashdod. *Hesder* students combine Torah study in yeshiva with military service. At one point in his service, Dov met Talia's father, and despite the age gap, a fruitful dialogue developed between them on questions of Judaism and Zionism, values and education. When Dov returned from his reserve duty, Talia's father suggested to his daughter that she correspond with Dov. Talia accepted this suggestion happily, since during that period she was exposed to Judaism through the seminars of Gesher (an organization that sponsors programs to bridge the gap between religious and secular Israelis and strengthen Jewish identity), in which she met with religious youth. These encounters awoke in Talia many questions that she wanted to clarify, and her father's suggestion came at the right time.

Dov and Talia corresponded for two years, during 1972 and 1973. Dov was in his second and third years of the *hesder* program, during which time he both studied in yeshiva and completed his military service. Talia was in eleventh and twelfth grade, completing high school and awaiting military induction.

The letters reveal the rich spiritual worlds of Dov and Talia and establish a bridge of understanding between these two young people who came from such different backgrounds. Their correspondence reveals commonalities but also the

---

[1] Talia is a made-up name. Her real name was not used out of a wish to honor her privacy.

profound gaps between the worlds of a yeshiva student and a girl from a secular kibbutz. Despite the gaps and the serious arguments, the intensive correspondence continued right up until Dov's death in the Yom Kippur War.

Dov became famous as the hero of the novel by Rabbi Haim Sabato, *Adjusting Sights* (in the Israeli movie based on the book he is called David). With the release of the book and the movie, many became interested in the character of Dov, a few strands of which are sketched by Rabbi Sabato in his book. But nothing can tell us as much about Dov's greatness as his letters to Talia. The memory of Dov's impressive personality accompanies his friends and acquaintances to this very day, despite the many years that have passed since he fell in battle. On the thirtieth anniversary of the Yom Kippur War, we, his family and friends, decided to publish for the first time the correspondence between Talia and Dov in its entirety, with only light editorial adjustments and supplementary footnotes to clarify the letters. We hope that this translated edition of the book will familiarize English-speaking readers with the world of *hesder* yeshiva students, who are known for the prominent role they played in the Yom Kippur War. We also hope the book will increase understanding between the many different streams making up the Jewish people, and that they will follow the path of Dov and Talia: the path of dialogue and communication rather than confrontation.

We hope that Dov's character will continue to illuminate our national persona, just as his own short life illuminated his surroundings with the light of kindness and great love – the love of God, the love of the Torah of Israel, the love of the people and land of Israel, and the love of all that is humane and worthwhile.

Hagi Ben-Artzi

The Letters

Dear Dov,

You must be surprised to have received a letter from a girl you don't know. So here's the story behind the letter: A number of months ago, a good friend of mine suggested that I sign up for a Gesher seminar. In case you haven't heard about it, Gesher is a recently established organization that sets up meetings between religious and secular youth. On our kibbutz, we don't have contact with religious kids, and we don't even have religious teachers in our school. Everything we know about religious people comes from newspapers and the radio. Although I have no intention of becoming religious, I decided, out of curiosity, to attend a seminar in order to get to know religious youth and to hear firsthand about their lives.

The meeting with them was really interesting, even fascinating. We learned a lot of things we hadn't known about the lives of religious Jews. This meeting got me asking a lot of questions about things I had seen or heard and not understood. When I got home, I tried to get answers to my questions from both my teachers and my parents – and in general, I didn't succeed. Almost all of them grew up on kibbutzim, and they too are unfamiliar with the lives of religious Jews. Although my parents came from religious families in Europe, both of them made aliya as children after the Holocaust, in which almost all their relatives were murdered. They barely recall anything from their childhoods, and the little they do remember they can't explain to me.

Recently my father returned from reserve duty on the Golan Heights, and he told me that he met a wonderful religious boy there who surprised him with the answers he gave about Judaism. My father told me that you are a bookworm who loves both books about Judaism and scientific encyclopedias, and that your answers are really on target. My father then said, "Instead of bugging me with your questions, write to him, and for sure he will answer you a lot better than I can." After struggling with this for several days (how can I possibly write to a boy that I've never met?) I decided to be brash and write you.

I hope you will give me a little bit of your time (I understand that you hesder students are very busy, since you both study and serve in the army) and answer several questions I have. The seminar I participated in got me asking a lot of questions, and I don't want to bombard you with them in my first letter (and anyway, you haven't yet agreed to answer me). All the same, I want to raise at least one question that has been bothering me since the seminar. At the end of every day at the seminar, after long hours of discussions and arguments, we would go out on the lawn of Kibbutz Kfar Etzion and dance wildly to Hasidic music. We really needed to break loose a little, to let ourselves go.

The Hasidic songs were mostly new for the nonreligious among us, but they had a really nice beat and they made you move. We were surprised that all the dancing was separate, with the boys in one circle and the girls in another. One time on television I saw a Hasidic wedding in which the men danced in one part of the hall and the women on the other side. I had always thought, though, that the Modern Orthodox (or the Dati Leumi [National Religious], as you call yourselves) don't keep up this primitive separation. In the age of equality of women, it's humiliating and insulting that this separation is maintained, as if we are impure or dirty and it is forbidden to touch us.

I hope you aren't offended by my blunt style and that it won't stop you from answering me. I write from the heart what I feel, and I don't mean to hurt you.

There. I've written enough, certainly for the first time. I hope you'll take my questions seriously, and that you are open even to hard questions, like my father said you are.

Thanks in advance,

Talia

ב"ה

28 HESHVAN 1971 [NOVEMBER 16, 1971][1]

Dear Talia,

I was happy to receive your letter, and I was even expecting it. When I said goodbye to your father at the end of my reserve duty, he told me he had a daughter who was becoming interested in Judaism after taking part in a seminar. I promised him that if you wrote me I would do my best to answer you, taking my limitations into account. I want to emphasize those last words about my limitations, because they reflect my true feelings. I grew up in a religious environment, I studied in religious educational institutions, and I never tried my skills at explaining Judaism to a secular public. I believe that it is our duty to do this, and to devote our best energies to this pursuit. But I, personally, have no experience doing this. In this context, I want to ask your permission to show your letters to my good friend, who has himself come from the secular world. He became religious a few years ago, and this year he left the yeshiva where I study and moved to Yeshivat Mercaz HaRav in Jerusalem to study the writings of Rabbi Abraham Isaac Kook.[2] My friend gives a lot of lectures to nonreligious people, and I want to get advice from him about your questions.

I do want to address the question you raised in your letter about separate dancing for boys and girls. You were right in starting precisely with this question. In my view, separation between men and women and between boys and girls is an essential part of Jewish culture: separate dancing, separate outings, separate education... In recent generations, Western culture has moved in precisely the opposite direction: coeducational schools, mixed recreation, and even mixed swimming (with scantily clad bathers). When you compare the two cultures, I

---

[1] In his letters, Dov used Hebrew dates. The secular dates were inserted by the editor.

[2] Rabbi Kook was the first chief rabbi in the land of Israel about eighty years ago. He is considered the father of religious Zionism from a philosophical standpoint.

5

think you can understand the logic behind the policy of separation. In religious and haredi society, the family structure is generally stable and long-lasting, and the incidence of divorce is very low. By contrast, in Western society, the family unit is collapsing, and the divorce statistics are frightening. As far as I know, about a third of the couples in America and Europe get divorced. Think about it: every third family falls apart.[3] We in Israel are not far behind, with one couple in five divorcing.[4] Such a high percentage of broken families, with the children being cut off in such a cruel way from one of their natural parents, constitutes a real social crisis.

I see a connection between secular society's having broken down all the barriers between men and women and the modern family's disintegration. I think a society interested in preserving the stability of the family must preserve fences regarding male-female relations outside the family unit. In Jewish tradition, this network of limitations is called *tzniyut*, modesty. I am sure this system contains nothing harmful or insulting to women. To the contrary, precisely the women who live according to the rules of modesty maintain happy family lives.

I think I've written enough for a first letter. In any event, I'd like to encourage you to keep writing and asking questions with the same candor you did in your first letter. You haven't hurt or insulted me. It's your right – or rather, your duty – to express everything you feel about the religious world that you encountered.

I'd like you to tell me a bit about your kibbutz, your studies, and especially what you learn about Judaism.

Sincerely,

Dov

---

[3] The divorce rate that Dov mentions refers to the 1970s. Today the divorce rate is between 40 percent and 50 percent in North America and 70 percent in Scandinavia.

[4] The divorce rate in Israel in 2002 was one in three (32 percent).

November 28, 1971

Dear Dov,

I was happy about your speedy reply and your willingness to relate seriously to a nudnik you don't know.

As far as your asking permission to get advice from your friend who became religious, I allow it, but I ask you not to show my letters to anyone. You can tell your friend about my questions, but the letters are personal and meant only for you.

I'd like to address your answer about the separate dancing at the Gesher seminar. I think you didn't answer my question. I asked you about high school kids dancing, and you wrote about families and divorce rates. What's the connection? My friends and I aren't even married, and we certainly aren't getting divorced yet.

I agree that the state of the family in the modern world is worrisome. On the kibbutz as well, several couples have gotten divorced, and my friend, whose father left the kibbutz after he and his wife divorced, really misses him. But what does that have to do with the recreational activities of young, unmarried people who want to have fun together? At our school we've got a folk dance club, with both boys and girls as members, and you can't imagine what fun it is to dance together. You religious people just don't know what you're missing!

You asked about Jewish studies in our school. It's like this: we study a lot of Bible, five hours a week, plus Jewish history and Hebrew literature. I really like what we study in history, but the Bible classes are really boring. Our teacher is pretty old, and he's always making comparisons between the Bible and ancient Egyptian and Babylonian writings. Right now we're learning Job, which has a lot of hard words. I can read a whole chapter and not understand a thing. Our teacher explains every word according to all sorts of ancient Semitic languages, and it really doesn't interest me.

Actually, the story at the beginning of the book was interesting, but also strange. How could God bring such tragedies on a righteous man just to test him? That seems illogical and unfair to me. I asked our teacher about that, but he gave me a complicated answer that I didn't understand at all. Maybe you can explain God's strange behavior in a clearer way.

My friends are starting to get angry with me because the light on my night table is keeping them awake.[1]

Good night,

Talia

P.S. What's the name of your friend who you go to for advice?

ב"ה

21 KISLEV 5732 [DECEMBER 9, 1971]

Dear Talia,

I've decided to answer you before Hanukkah, so that during your vacation you'll be able to read my letter and answer it.

First of all, I want to address your confusion as far as my answer regarding separation of men and women. You ask – and your question seems justified – what does the mixed dancing of teenagers before marriage have to do with the stability of the family and divorce rates? After all, we can distinguish between social behavior before marriage and behavior after marriage. I too struggled greatly with this question in high school, when I was in Bnei Akiva and mixed dancing was the subject of stormy debate. I took this question to one of my teachers at my yeshiva high school, Netiv Meir. This man was not only an expert in Torah but had a broad general education as well (in yeshiva we call our Torah teachers *ramim*, an acronym for the Aramaic expression *resh metivta*, i.e., head of a house of study). He referred me to a book on social psychology (I think the book was called Window on Social Psychology), where I read something

---

[1] Talia lived in a separate apartment on the kibbutz with other girls.

very interesting. All the research in this sphere supports the claim that the habits and behavioral norms of teenagers fashion our behavior for the rest of our lives. Also, the moral tracts I read, such as Michtav Me'Eliyahu by Rabbi Dessler, and Alei Shur by Rabbi Wolbe, emphasize the connection between *girsa d'yankuta* [knowledge acquired in childhood], which includes everything we learned and did when we were young, and our way of life and mode of thought when we are adults. (Don't be put off by all the rabbis I mention. Maybe sometime you'll have a chance to study their books, and you'll see that they say very wise and logical things.)

Do you really think a person who as a kid got used to mixed dancing or mixed swimming will suddenly stop all that the day after his wedding? Do you really think someone who swapped mates before marriage like people change shoes (and sometimes like people change socks) will in one fell swoop change his habits and lifestyle after marriage? After all, you too agree (or so I understand from your letter) that mixed society, in which there is intensive contact between men and women after marriage, is liable to endanger the stability of the family unit.

In a word, if you agree that the rules of separation and modesty between men and women are important to preserving the family's well-being and stability, then you have to apply them to life before marriage as well, and not just to married people.

I was happy to read that you learn a lot of Bible. I too try to learn at least a chapter of the Bible every day, in addition to the week's Torah portion. I agree with you that studying Bible the way you study archaeological findings is boring. For me, every chapter, every verse of the Bible tells me what I have to do and how I have to live as a good Jew, here and now. That's how I try to learn the Bible. For me, the Bible is a book about real life and not just ancient literature, because I believe that the Bible reveals to man God's word, which is eternal, just as God is eternal.

Man's soul is eternal as well, since man was created "in the image of God." Many biblical verses talk about the divine nature of the soul: "The life-breath of man is the lamp of the Lord" (Proverbs 20:27), and "It is part of God above" (Job 31:2). This, I believe, is the real answer to your question about the test in the book of Job. Our sages teach us that man's life in this world is like a corridor leading to the World to Come, where the soul lives on forever. The trials that God sends us, with all of their concomitant pain and suffering, require us to rise spiritually, to overcome our weaknesses, to discover the enormity of our faith. All this increases the power of the soul, or in our sages' words, "increases our reward in the World to Come." That reward is not something external and separate from the soul, like a sort of compensation. Rather, it constitutes the quality of our eternal lives, a quality that is determined by the level of our faith and self-sacrifice here on this earth.

There, I've written enough. The night is almost over, and soon they will come to wake me up for Shaharit [morning prayer services]. I've got to catch some shut-eye. Otherwise, I won't be able to learn tomorrow.

Take care,

Dov

P.S. The name of my friend whom I get advice from about your letters is Hagi Ben-Artzi.

DECEMBER 22, 1971

Dear Dov,

During my Hanukkah break, I had a lot of free time and I read your letter several times. I was surprised to discover that you also read psychology books. I thought that in yeshiva you only read holy books.

I agree with you that there is a connection between our behavioral patterns before marriage and our way of life as married people. But unlike what you assume, I don't agree that there's anything bad about married people living in a mixed society. Do you really think families break up because they go swimming at a coed beach, that couples get divorced because of a lively dance party? These things just bring happiness to our lives, and we are in such great need of a little happiness. Even at the Gesher seminar there was a lecturer who spoke about the joy of the Hasidic movement. Every evening, with great enthusiasm, we sang this song (I think by Rabbi Nahman of Breslov), "It is a great mitzva to be happy always." What's bad about the joy of life? The time I have the most fun is at the pool during summer vacation, and my happiest moments are at my school's folk dance classes and at the evening kibbutz sing-alongs.

Do you know why couples get divorced? It's because they're not suited to one another. Sometimes that incompatibility is psychological, and sometimes it's physical. In my view, it's actually a good thing that couples who aren't suited to each other, and don't get along together, get divorced instead of turning their lives into a constant hell. Maybe precisely the low divorce rate in religious society attests to their running away from courageously confronting the real problems with the institution of marriage. They repress their problems due to the social stigma against divorced people. I claim that divorced people can be wonderful people who simply haven't found the appropriate mate for their character and personality. In such situations, I think it's better to get divorced than to sweep the problems under the carpet.

Enough. It gives me the creeps to write so many times about divorce. Luckily for me, I live in a wonderful family, and my parents get along great (except for small arguments here and there).

I brought your answer about the trials in the book of Job to my Bible teacher. He really laughed at the answer, and he said that the World to Come is never mentioned in the book of Job. Job does not know about the World to Come, and the author of the book does not use this belief to answer the problem of "the righteous sufferer." Maybe you've got a different answer?

I've got to tell you about a big argument that took place in my class before Hanukkah. My history teacher said that she doesn't light Hanukkah candles, because the Maccabees were extremists and fanatics, and had they lived in our times, they would certainly have fought against the secular. Most students in the class agreed with her, but some were opposed, saying that the Maccabees fought for the independence of the Jewish people and established a state, so we identify with them and celebrate Hanukkah. There was a big argument, which we continued that night as well. I, personally, love to read about the wars of the Maccabees and their heroic deeds, but I really didn't have so much to answer to those who told me that the Maccabees wouldn't have let me travel on Shabbat. I would be very happy to hear where you stand in this debate.

Tomorrow, we are starting class again, and I still have a lot of homework, so I'd better sign off here.

Good night,

Looking forward to your prompt response,

Talia

ב"ה

19 TEVET 5732 [JANUARY 6, 1972]

Dear Talia,

Another week is ending, and tomorrow I'm going home for an "off-Shabbat."[1] I haven't seen my family in almost three weeks, since Hanukkah, and I really miss them. My mother would like me to come home every Shabbat, but it's hard for me to miss out

---

[1] The *hesder* yeshiva students usually spend Shabbat, the Sabbath, in their yeshivot, but occasionally go home to spend the Sabbath with their families.

on Sabbaths at the yeshiva, since they are so spiritually uplifting. Yet, honoring one's parents is a mitzva from the Torah as well, so the compromise is something like spending Shabbat at home once every two or three weeks.

I, like you, am not married, so I can't answer your questions based on personal experience but only based on the moral tracts that I read, and conversations with my teachers in yeshiva (one of my teachers, who until recently was the *mashgiah* [spiritual guidance counselor] of the yeshiva, is a psychologist by practice, and his talks have been based not only on books on ethics but also on science and psychology books).[1]

In all of the books on ethics, constant reference is made to our sages' utterance in the Talmud that "there is no guardian against unchastity." What this expression means is that nobody can rely on himself when it comes to overcoming sexual urges, so Jewish law forbids us to expose ourselves to sexual temptation when we are liable to fall prey to it.

Do you think that a boss who stays at work with his secretary until the late hours of the evening is not liable to find himself, before he knows it, in a tempestuous romance? Do you think that a man who goes swimming at the pool and encounters the same beautiful woman there every night (with her almost naked) is not liable to find himself in her bed as well?

Time and again our sages warned us, "There is no guardian against unchastity," and we are forbidden to place ourselves in an impossible test whose results are tragic (generally, with the family falling apart). You are trying to describe some innocent picture of people sitting around and singing together. What's wrong with that, you justifiably ask. But let's not be naive. You surely know that it doesn't end with that. Western society today (and Israeli society is part of that culture), with all its recreational and entertainment milieus, has reached a much more extreme state of permissiveness. All

---

[1] The reference is to Rabbi Chaim Lipschitz, who was the spiritual guidance counselor of Yeshivat Kerem B'Yavneh until 1972. Then he established the Sadnat Enosh (human workshop) Institute in Jerusalem.

the world literature describes in endless novels this process of moving from "simple" friendship and "wholesome" recreation to betrayal and adultery. Only recently I read Boris Pasternak's novel *Dr. Zhivago* (Hagi suggested that I also see the movie, but after thinking about this briefly, I decided to make do with the book). The book describes in a really astonishing manner how betrayal starts from small things that look innocent and entirely unproblematic. Apparently, Talia, you can't have your cake and eat it too. You can't both believe in the importance of family and also believe in a Western-style, mixed society. It's a solid fact: wherever the traditional rules of modesty have been breached, the family unit has been breached as well, and cases of divorce increase at an alarming rate.

Your question about the Maccabees led me back to my history books to check out what precisely happened during the period of the rebellion. I took up Simon Dubnov's book about the Second Temple period (this is one in a series of eight or nine books about the whole history of the Jewish people), and something interesting became clear to me. The struggle between the Hellenists, who to some extent adopted Greek culture, and the righteous adherents, who remained faithful to the tradition of Israel, had been going on for at least 150 years before the rebellion (from the conquests of Alexander the Great, the Greek leader who conquered the whole ancient world and brought Greek culture even to the land of Israel). This struggle bore a cultural, nonviolent stamp as long as the Hellenists used explanation and persuasion. Things changed dramatically in the days of Antiochus IV Epiphanes. He tried to force Greek culture on the Jewish people, and accompanied this attempt with frightening decrees against religion, called, in Jewish tradition, "Antiochus's decrees." Maccabees I and II portray a shocking picture of women and children taken out to be executed because they fulfilled the mitzva of circumcision, and old men hanged in the streets because they were caught red-handed with Torah scrolls.

Dubnov writes that according to Maccabees I and II, and other sources, apparently some of the Hellenists cooperated with Antiochus and with his decrees, turning in Jews who fulfilled mitzvot in secret. Consider how shocking it is that Jews turned in their fellow Jews when all they wanted to do was to study our nation's Torah and preserve our heritage. Only then did the Maccabee revolt break out. This was an enormously justified rebellion against heinous, cruel religious coercion. The Maccabees fought for religious freedom, so you, of all people, have all the reasons in the world to identify with them and to light Hanukkah candles in order to celebrate their victory. This is a victory of freedom over coercion, of loyalty over betrayal, of faith over cynicism, of heroism over cowardice. Don't you believe in all these values?

True, they learned Torah and kept Shabbat and ate only kosher food in accordance with Jewish tradition. But they didn't harm or restrict in any way their brethren who ate pork and violated Shabbat, as long as the Hellenists did not try to force assimilation upon them.

In any event, thanks to your question, I was privileged this year to refresh my knowledge about the Maccabee revolt, and Hanukkah this year was more meaningful for me than in previous years.

I see that soon Shaharit will be starting, and I want to finish. (I wrote this letter in the study hall where I stayed to study all night with about ten other boys. Here in yeshiva, we call this custom of studying all night *mishmar* [night watch], at the end of which we pray *vatikin*, meaning that we time our morning prayers to reach their climax precisely at sunrise.)

The rest of our discussion on the book of Job will have to wait for my next letter, which I hope will be sent soon (that depends on your next letter).

So, this time I'm signing off with "good morning" wishes and a *Shabbat shalom* [peaceful Sabbath],

Dov

15

JANUARY 18, 1972

Dear Dov,

I wanted to write you as soon as I got your letter, but we had several big tests, which forced me to push off my answer by several days. I hope you won't learn from me and will continue to write and to answer my questions without delays and excuses. Your letters are really interesting and I wait for them with baited breath.

I was sorry to read in your letter that you had decided not to see the movie *Dr. Zhivago*. It's really a wonderful movie about a great and true love. I don't understand what is bad about love between a married man and a married woman. True, it often ends with the lovers' previous families breaking up, but I believe that love is the greatest, most important thing in life. Do you believe there is anything greater? A person has to pursue his love even if it distances him from other important things.

I assume you know that in the last several years, since the Six-Day War, a lot of volunteers, male and female, have been coming to my kibbutz from all over the world to express their support for the State of Israel. Several kibbutz members fell in love with volunteers and married them, and left Israel to live with their loves abroad. There have been a lot of arguments about these couples who left the kibbutz and Israel, and many have condemned them and even suggested ostracizing them. I, however, have supported them, because in my eyes, nothing is more right than pursuing love.

I ask of you, Dov, don't avoid this topic. Write back to me honestly and candidly about whether you agree with me or think there are things more important than love, things that make it worth giving up love.

This time I am going to make due with a short letter, because tomorrow I've got a math test, and being as lazy as I am, I haven't even started studying.

So in the meantime take care,

Talia

ב"ה

14 SHVAT 5732 [JANUARY 30, 1972]

Dear Talia,

Just got back to my room from a "Seder Tu B'Shvat"[1] held in the yeshiva dining room. This is a very special meal, consisting entirely of the fruits of Eretz Yisrael, the land of Israel. The entire evening was dedicated to Eretz Yisrael, with rabbinic expositions and sermons about Eretz Yisrael in the Bible, Jewish law, and Jewish lore. There was also a guest lecturer who spoke about the immigration of Jews to Eretz Yisrael in the Middle Ages. I think there was something very moving about his lecture. Eretz Yisrael during the Middle Ages was parched and desolate, with very few Jewish inhabitants. Even so, Jews never stopped coming to it even during the most difficult times – Ramban and Rabbi Yehuda HaLevi, Rabbi Yehiel of Paris and Rabbi Ovadia of Bartenura[2] and many more. What astounding loyalty on the part of Jews for their ancient homeland, even after hundreds of years of exile and being cut off from it. The lecturer mentioned the book *HaMa'avak L'Dorot* [Struggle over generations] by Professor Dinur,[3] which includes much material on this topic. On my next break, possibly on Purim, I hope to go to the National Library and to borrow this book.

In your next letter, tell me a bit about how your kibbutz marks Tu B'Shvat. Do you, too, have something like our "Seder Tu B'Shvat"?

You knocked me off balance with your comments about love, and I don't intend to avoid them. As a believing, observant

---

[1] Tu B'Shvat, the fifteenth of the Hebrew month of Shvat, is a holiday celebrating the "New Year for the trees." Some people observe it with a "seder," or special meal, as Dov describes.

[2] Great Torah sages of the Jewish people, especially the first two.

[3] Ben-Zion Dinur, 1884–1973: a noted Zionist educator and later Israeli politician who was born into a traditional Ukrainian family but departed from his family's religious traditions in favor of the worldview of the Haskala ("Enlightenment").

Jew, I will not marry, God forbid, a non-Jewish woman, even if
I fall in love with her. As a believing Jew, I will not, God forbid,
carry on a romance with a married woman, no matter how
enchanting she is. For me, loyalty to a God that I believe in, and
in the Torah that He gave me, overrides loyalty to the strongest
love emotions possible (obviously I am talking about when the
two conflict). The Genesis story of Isaac being bound as a sacrifice offers the strongest expression I know of regarding this
difficult decision in situations of conflict and contradiction.

I admit that it is hard for someone who does not believe
in God to accept this preference. On the other hand, however, it
is hard for a believer not to agree with this principle.

God, Who created us and taught us how to live, so that
we can fulfill our mission in the world as human beings and
our destiny as Jews, warns us not to be swept away by our emotions and passions. Twice a day every religious Jew recites the
Shema,[4] which ends with the warning: "Do not stray after
your heart (emotions, love) and your eyes (beauty, aesthet-
ics), which in the past have led you to immorality.... *Be holy to
your God!*" (Numbers 15:39–40). (I am sure that you learned
something about the prayer book and that you are familiar
with the Shema.) According to this verse, holiness means man's
being loyal to God, overcoming his emotions, proclivities, and
desires, which are liable to pull him in directions that go against
the Torah.

Look, Talia, I don't think a person who follows his emotions is going to be a happier person. In the end, all love is worn
down by routine and the passage of time. And then what? Will
you look for a new love, which will likewise grow old after several months or years? In this way, people are dragged from one
romance to another, from one love to another, without any
anchor, without any stability or continuity. In America, where
your outlook is very widespread, there are already lots of people
who have gotten divorced twice or three times or four... Do

---

[4] The Shema, the central prayer of Judaism, contains passages from
Deuteronomy (6:4–9, 11:13–21) and Numbers (15:37–41).

you think these people are happier than those who remain faithful to their first love, who don't look for adventures and excitement, but stubbornly and steadfastly build a common life together? I think the latter group achieves a much greater, truer love than those who "flutter" from flower to flower, from one mate to the next.

True, remaining faithful to one wife requires a lot of work, investment, constancy, and self-sacrifice, but I believe that at the end of the day, this is the real love, not the passing excitement of falling in love, today with one woman and tomorrow with another. I recently read a book by a well-known American psychologist who presents precisely this outlook. The book is called *The Art of Loving* and it was written by Erich Fromm. I highly recommend it. He too distinguishes between the momentary, superficial excitement of falling in love, devoid of deeper meaning, and true love, which a couple builds together through ongoing toil and psychological investment over many years. Erich Fromm harshly criticizes Western society, which highly values romantic, superficial love at the expense of the deeper kind that demands a long-term investment.

Obviously, the deeper love that a couple builds together has its ups and downs, crises and disappointments, together with wonderful heights of supreme joy. Yet whoever despairs at every crisis, whoever seeks his consolation, whenever there is a difficult moment, in the arms of another woman, will clearly not be able to persevere and ultimately harvest the fruits of true love.

The great wisdom of Jewish law is that it aims to distance man from situations in which he will be torn between love and Torah. One way it achieves this is through all the rules about modesty, which I wrote a lot about in our previous letters. If we keep married men and women apart, we lessen the chances that love will develop that will tear them away from their spouses. If we distance Jews and non-Jews and limit the social encounters between them, we thereby lessen the chances that a Jewish man or woman will fall in love with a non-Jew. As is well known, the wise person is one who avoids becoming involved with problems that ten wise men will find hard to solve.

I also owe you an answer about the book of Job, which I didn't manage to fit into my last letter. I think your Bible teacher is right and the World to Come is not mentioned in that book. I think, however, that that is exactly Job's problem, that he does not believe in man's immortality after his physical death. He describes death as the absolute end of man: "Man born of woman is short-lived and sated with trouble.... Mortals languish and die; Man expires; where is he?" (Job 14:10). By contrast, a tree, even if it is chopped down, can produce new branches: "There is hope for a tree. If it is cut down it will renew itself. Its shoots will not cease" (ibid., 7).

I argue (I think I saw this in Rabbi Yaakobson's work *L'she'elat HaGmul BaMikra* [On the question of reward in Scripture]) that the book of Job was included in the Bible to show what despair man can fall into if he does not recognize belief in the World to Come or immortality after death. Without this faith, there truly is no justice, no fair reward and punishment. Instead, the righteous suffer and the wicked prosper. Then there is not any reason for our entire lives either, as King Solomon said, "Utter futility! All is futile" (Ecclesiastes 1:2). Faith in a World to Come following death changes man's perspective on life and on justice entirely. Life in this world is just a small portion of the immortality of man's divine soul, and seeing this one portion presents a totally distorted picture.

Imagine being shown a picture of five men bending over a tiny infant and cutting its body. Presumably you would be shocked. But this picture is part of a movie telling the story of five physicians struggling to save the life of a little boy suffering from a serious illness. This, in my view, is the background behind Job's great cry, from which he calms down only after God appears to him out of the storm and reveals to him the secret of man's immortality. Man can never arrive at this secret through his own intellect. Rather, a divine revelation is required for man to get the whole picture. Bring this answer to your Bible teacher and write me what he responds.

It's already very late and sleep is getting the better of me. I feel like I've written enough to give you food for thought.

Looking forward to your response,

Dov

FEBRUARY 15, 1972

Dear Dov,

I am really jealous of the way you celebrated Tu B'Shvat. You religious people really know how to make a nice meal at every opportunity. We, by contrast, worked hard on Tu B'Shvat. They took us to plant trees on some "frozen tundra" in the Upper Galilee. We worked all day almost without stopping. Everybody managed to plant dozens of saplings.

Reward time came in the afternoon. We made a wonderful picnic in some little valley that had a beautiful spring. They brought a truck from the kibbutz full of food. We had a cookout, and some of the kids even went rappelling from one of the cliffs. To me it looked too scary, so I refused to take part, but there were girls braver than me who did take part.

Luckily for us we don't have any rabbis here like you do in your yeshiva. For sure they would have given some sort of lecture about the land of Israel during the picnic. Our teachers who accompanied us throughout the day seemed to be enjoying a day off. I don't think they had any desire to teach anything.

I told my Bible teacher what you told me about the book of Job, and once again, he really split his sides laughing. He said he agrees with you that Job didn't recognize the existence of life after death, but he disagrees with you that at the end of the book faith in the World to Come makes an appearance. Job concedes only because God tells him that he doesn't understand anything, and therefore he also has no chance of understanding

God's behavior. During my Bible class, I looked through the book of Job (I don't listen much in that class anyway) and I really did see that at the end of the book, Job doesn't say anything about the World to Come. He just says something unclear: "Therefore, I recant and relent, being but dust and ashes" (Job 42:6). How do you understand that sentence?

This time I'm really proud of myself, because I wasn't lazy. I went to the school library and got out the book you recommended: *The Art of Loving.* I began reading it toward evening and I couldn't put it down. I finished it at two in the morning and the next day I slept through all my classes. That's really a great book. I think he succeeds in making the case that there's a big difference between the initial, superficial excitement of falling in love and real love. I really like Fromm's statement that we love falling in love but not loving itself. He really aroused in me a lot of thoughts about our lives: Aren't we mixing up the main thing with what is secondary?[1]

But I was against some things he said. It's very nice to invest toil and effort in marriage and in building a relationship. But what happens if it doesn't work? What happens if there's no compatibility, and then all that toil is in vain? Why not break up such relationships immediately? Why waste years on something unworkable?

My mother once told me that the religious don't get divorced because there is a very strong social stigma against divorce. So what do you think is better – living a perpetual hell with an incompatible person, or breaking up and trying to start over with someone else? Anyway, I really thank you for your suggestion. I'd be happy if you continued recommending more good books that you've read (but not books by rabbis).

Looking forward to your answer,

Good night and see you,

Talia

---

[1] This is a reference to the Talmudic dictum not to confuse a thing of primary importance with a thing of secondary importance.

P.S. Last night I read the book again, and I really think it's a great book. Thank you.

ב"ה

10 ADAR I 5732 [FEBRUARY 25, 1972]

Dear Talia,

Hagi (the friend that I consult with regarding your letters) has come for a visit to the yeshiva.[1] He said he misses the crowd he studied with and did the army with for almost four years. Hopefully he will be with us from Shabbat Zachor until Shushan Purim (the Shabbat before Purim is called Shabbat Zachor because that Shabbat we read the Torah section in which we are commanded, "Remember [*zachor*] what Amalek did to you." Shushan Purim is the day Purim is celebrated in Jerusalem [one day after the rest of the country celebrates the holiday]. He will return to Mercaz HaRav to celebrate Jerusalem's Purim.)

We talked a lot about the book of Job and about your questions (or, more precisely, your teacher's questions). Hagi showed me that the Rambam, in his *Guide for the Perplexed* (III:23) explains the words "dust and ashes" as relating to all the material things in this world. When Job says, "Therefore, I recant and relent, being but dust and ashes," he means that there is no importance to man's physical life, but only to his eternal life, the spiritual life of the soul (what Rambam calls the *sechel*). We looked for sources for Rambam's interpretation, and we found several Midrashim that explain this verse along the same lines.

Oops, I'm starting to write you as though you were a yeshiva guy. So I apologize that I didn't start with something about the Rambam. He was the leader of Egyptian Jewry eight hundred years ago, an authority in Jewish law, a philosopher, and

---

[1] At that time Hagi was studying in Yeshivat Mercaz HaRav in Jerusalem, and he visited Kerem B'Yavneh, where he had completed the *hesder* program.

a prominent physician. The book I mentioned, *Guide for the Perplexed*, is the most important book he wrote in the realm of philosophy, and one of the most important Jewish philosophy books of all times. We in yeshiva study his Jewish legal writings a great deal, his *Mishne Torah* and his *Perush LaMishna*, but Hagi studies many philosophical works. In your school, do you study something about Rambam or about his works?

I was really happy to read in your letter that you, like me, enjoyed the book *The Art of Loving*. For me too this is one of the most significant books that I have read. It is clear to me that Erich Fromm does not mean we have to remain stuck all our lives with someone we don't get along with. Neither is that the position of Jewish law, which, as you know, permits divorce and sometimes even requires it. The big question he raises is this: How does one relate to the difficulties and crises that crop up in every good family? Do we collapse and escape, looking for a "new fling," or do we confront the problem and try to rebuild from there, uncovering new strengths? It's no great art to break down and say "It didn't work" instead of mustering all of one's psychological resources to overcome the difficulties. I believe that precisely following such a confrontation we achieve love on a much higher plane than before the difficulties.

There is a chapter in *The Art of Loving* (you must certainly recall it; after all, you read it twice – good for you!), in which Erich Fromm goes even further. He says that sometimes people escape from a marriage not due to objective difficulties but out of a constant search for new excitement. Life with one person becomes routine after a few years, and the need arises to relive the experience of first falling in love. By then, this experience is hard to capture with a familiar, "boring" person, so…the person cheats on his spouse. It's not the difficulties that create the cheating, but the cheating that creates the difficulties, for generally, most couples get divorced as a result. In my opinion, Fromm doesn't really offer a solution to this basic problem, but Judaism does have a wonderful, indeed amazing solution.

Now you are probably waiting anxiously to hear what amazing solution I'm talking about, but I am going to leave you in suspense until my next letter. I am simply dying of fatigue (all evening I talked and studied with Hagi), and now it's almost three o'clock in the morning. Tomorrow is "Shabbat Zachor," and our custom here in yeshiva is to dance on this Shabbat until late. I have to sleep a bit so that I will have the energy to dance.

So good night,

Take care,

Dov

FEBRUARY 27, 1972

Dear Dov,

I haven't yet received your response to my last letter, but I'm writing you again anyway. With all my excitement over Erich Fromm's book, I forgot to answer your last letter from Tu B'Shvat. It contained something in it that really got me angry and even insulted me.

You write that as a believer, you cannot follow your love and marry, for example, a non-Jewish girl. I, too, define myself as a believer. I, too, believe in God. But the God I believe in created man with emotions, and He certainly wants us to flow with them. After all, that's how He created us, so why say no to our natural emotions? The God I believe in wants us to be loyal to our nature, to the energies that He granted us, and not to all sorts of strange demands by rabbis from thousands of years ago. What is your opinion about this belief? I know your belief is different from mine, but I'm not willing to have someone define me as a nonbeliever.

I am waiting for your response both to this letter and to my last letter.

Sincerely yours,

Talia

MARCH 3, 1972

Dear Dov,

Today I received your letter and it really got me angry. You tell me Judaism has an amazing solution to the problem of boredom in marriage and you leave me hanging? That's really unfair! I tried to guess what you mean, but I couldn't think of anything that seems "amazing." Maybe you have some special prayer in mind that you say every night before you go to sleep? I really beg of you: this time don't leave me hanging and write soon!

I'm starting to like your interpretation of Job. The idea of "dust and ashes" relating to our lives here on earth seems right and true. I haven't yet had a chance to talk to my Bible teacher about your answer, but I assume that once more he will roll on the floor laughing, and will tell me that you don't interpret the Bible using Midrashim. Midrashim can't provide the straightforward meaning of the Bible. He always tells us that there is a Judaism of the Bible and a Judaism of the rabbis.

By the way, I've got news that you will certainly be happy to hear. I signed up with another friend for the Gesher seminar on Pesach. I feel like the Sukkot seminar opened up a window on a very interesting world that I was unfamiliar with before. Since that seminar, I have started to really want to learn about Judaism. Your letters, as well, strengthen that desire in me, because from every one of your letters, I discover new things that give me a great deal of food for thought. So at Pesach, I'll be at Kfar Etzion.[1] Until then, I hope to receive at least one letter from you (you now owe me answers to two letters).

All the best,

Talia

---

[1] A religious kibbutz in Judea.

ב"ה

27 Adar I 5732 [March 13, 1972]

Dear Talia,

I was really happy to read in your last letter that you had registered for another Gesher seminar. There's nothing like direct, firsthand knowledge. Books and letters can only supplement that. Maybe you'll meet Hagi there, because he told me that he will be a youth counselor at the Pesach seminar.

I know it was a bit "nasty" of me to leave you hanging. I apologize for that, but I wasn't sure whether to write you about the "secret" of marriage, since we're both still unmarried. In the end I decided our correspondence has to be frank and open, and I hope that it will be that way from your end as well.

You surely are aware that Judaism views sexual relations between husband and wife as a very significant component in building and fostering the relationship. If one spouse consistently refuses, or is incapable of having full and normal sexual relations, that is grounds for divorce. All the same, Jewish law forbids the couple to have any physical contact about two weeks out of every month (it varies between couples, but the minimum is twelve forbidden days). The forbidden time includes the days of the woman's period, plus seven more days after the end of her period. The Talmud in Tractate Nidda (a woman during her forbidden time is called a *nidda*) states that the goal of the prohibition is to refresh the couple's sex lives, and to prevent their sinking into routine and boredom. The cyclic nature of intimacy and distance facilitates renewed energies and longing, restores the couple to their courtship period before marriage, and transforms the monthly encounter to a time of renewed excitement. As Rabbi Meir (one of the greatest Mishnaic scholars) said: "Why did the Torah say that the *nidda* must wait a week? The husband, becoming used to his wife, may tire of her. Hence, the Torah said, Let her be forbidden to him for seven days so she can be dear to him as she was at the moment of their marriage."

Rabbi Meir is raising the issue of routine and erosion in married life, which have no solution but to create a cyclic pattern of prohibition and permission, intimacy and distance. I view this as a marvelous innovation, which I believe does not exist in any other religion. Sometimes I think this is yet one more proof that Judaism is not based on human wisdom, but on divine revelation.

I am interested in knowing if you knew anything about *taharat hamishpaha* (family purity, as it is called in the halachic literature). Does it seem to you like an effective approach, or does this too seem old-fashioned and primitive to you?

The God that I believe in worries about man and helps him to build a full, happy life, but the condition for this is the person's ability to restrain himself and to overcome his passions. The God that I believe in created man with good impulses and bad impulses. The good impulses have to be strengthened and nurtured, and the bad ones have to be restrained and blocked. We also have to know how to limit and balance our positive forces. The book of Proverbs teaches, "It is not good to eat much honey" (Proverbs 25:27). In a word, the God that I believe in gave us the Torah, which instructs us how to lead the ideal life. True, all our energies and drives were created by God, not so we would "flow with all our strengths," but so we would strike a balance between them and have control over them. According to the Jewish outlook, that is actually the greatest test man faces in this world. You are right that this is not the outlook of liberal Western culture, which generally tends toward permissiveness. But you can't call such an outlook the outlook of a believing person, since no religion thinks that this is what God wants of man.

In short, I accept and respect your wish to define yourself as a "believer," but I think you have to ask yourself if God only created the world with all its energies, or if He also gave us the

Torah, which guides us in how to make use of the energies that He created (a sort of manufacturer's user's guide).

In any event, one thing is clear to me now. My own energies are really gone, because it's almost two o'clock in the morning. I owe you an answer about the Bible and the Midrash, but that's for next time.

All the best,

Dov

P.S. Despite all I wrote, I was very happy to read that you define yourself as a believer.

MARCH 20, 1972

Dear Dov,

The truth is that you managed to surprise me. How simple, but how brilliant, is this rhythm of two weeks on and two weeks off! Actually, this cycle is based on the natural cycle of the woman, but it expands it from several days (the average length of the monthly cycle) to two weeks.

There is something I really didn't understand on this point. In your letter you quoted Rabbi Meir, who says that a *nidda* is impure for seven days, and not for two weeks, so where does the two weeks come from? Besides that, why call the woman *nidda* [literally, "ostracized"] and "impure"? All in all, she's in a state of her womb being cleansed and prepared for the possibility of a new pregnancy. That is a natural process with nothing "impure" or wrong about it.

I asked my mother if she knows what family purity is. She was really surprised and asked me where I had heard about it. I calmed her down that I hadn't learned about it in school but from your letters. She told me that actually most couples don't cohabit while the woman is having her period, but the whole matter of immersing in a *mikve*[1] seems old-fashioned and

---

[1] A ritual purification bath.

illogical to her. She told me that according to Jewish law, it's not enough to bathe or shower after one's cycle, but that one has to immerse in a *mikve*. She couldn't explain to me precisely what a *mikve* is, since she was only there one time, before her wedding, but I understood from her that it wasn't a particularly joyful experience for her. Maybe you can tell me a bit more about what a *mikve* is and why Jewish law is so insistent about immersion in one, and why bathing in a bathtub, which is so easy and hygienic, does not suffice.

I do not agree with you that this law of family purity proves that God gave the Torah. It's just as logical to say that Moses or some other wise man who wrote the Torah's laws was a true genius and he invented successful tricks for strengthening the couple and the family. Who says that something wise can't be human?

My friend, who is going with me to the Gesher seminar, has become a real nut about Jewish books. Yesterday she brought me a book by Joseph Schechter, *MiMada L'Emuna* [From science to faith], and she told me that I should read this book before the seminar. Her parents are really afraid that she will become religious and leave the kibbutz. I feel like I am really strong, and I don't have to fear that I might become religious. But I'm also annoyed with my school that they don't make it possible for us to learn more about Judaism, which is the culture of our people.

On that combative note I shall sign off.

Good night and write quickly,

Talia

ב"ה

12 NISAN 5732 [MARCH 27, 1972], QUNEITRA

Dear Talia,

This time I'm writing you from Quneitra[2] in the Golan Heights, and not from the yeshiva. They took us, all the students of the

---

[2] Largely abandoned city located in the now-demilitarized UN Disengagement

yeshiva, for "Operation Pesach" on army bases throughout Israel. All the *hesder* yeshiva students clean all the army base kitchens and make them kosher for Pesach. I was brought to the military police base in Quneitra, and for two days already, I have been working with the *kashrut*[1] supervisor of the base to make the kitchen kosher. The view here is magnificent. Just above Quneitra, the Hermon Mountains rise up, their caps still white from the winter snow. To the east, the Damascus valley stretches forth, all covered with fields of green.

Last night, together with several other soldiers, I hopped over to Kibbutz Merom Golan, which is in the area. The kibbutz looks really nice, with lawns and small gardens around the houses. It's a charming spot sitting between the black basalt mountains of the Golan. One of the kibbutzniks saw that I was religious, and he grabbed me for a short talk. "Why don't the religious establish more settlements on the Golan Heights?" he asked. "The Heights are really empty, and they are crying out for more inhabitants. What happened to the mitzva of settling the land of Israel?" I was a bit embarrassed, but I think he is right. We've got to bring thousands of inhabitants to the Golan Heights, to fill it up with life and with light.

I am still in yeshiva in the framework of my military service, but maybe after *hesder*, I'll be privileged to come up to the Golan Heights and take part in the settlement enterprise that is starting to develop here.

Just before I left for the Pesach operation, I received your letter. All your questions, as usual, are on target. Regarding the discrepancy between a week and two weeks, you were right in what you noticed. According to the Torah, the separation period is usually just a week, and only in relatively rare cases does it stretch to two weeks or more.

The forbidden period was expanded in accordance with our sages' decrees and the customs practiced by Jewish women. Today the law is that every woman has to count "seven clean

---

Observer Force Zone between Israel and Syria in the Golan Heights.

[1] *Kashrut* is the system of Jewish dietary laws.

days" at the end of her period, and then to immerse in a *mikve*, a kosher ritual bath, and only then can she cohabit again with her husband. A period of about two weeks is apparently the optimal length for renewing the couple's mutual attraction without demanding self-restraint beyond their limits. I am not yet married, and I cannot testify about this from personal experience, but one central fact speaks for itself: the framework of family purity has preserved the Jewish family for thousands of years under terrible conditions of exile and wandering as a fortress of stability and happiness. How painful it is that precisely when we've come back to our land and established ourselves politically and economically, the Jewish family faces a difficult crisis and so many families are breaking up. Don't you think that this is tied to the process of abandoning a religious way of life, which is, in my belief, the only recipe for a full and happy family life?

The *mikve* isn't something terrible, as you may have gotten the impression from your mother. Men don't immerse every month like women, but men do go to a kosher *mikve* at least once a year, on the day before Yom Kippur. Some go on other holidays too. I go several times a year and it's always a special, exalting experience. Every time I go, I recall the beautiful words of Rabbi Elimelekh Bar-Shaul (who was once the educational director of our yeshiva), who described the immersion experience as one of rebirth. As is well-known, the fetus is in water, the placenta fluid of the womb, and the person going to the *mikve* likewise emerges from the water like a person who has just been born. The birth experience, the feeling that after immersion you are like a person who has been reborn, is reinforced by the fact that according to Jewish law, the water in the *mikve* consists of natural rainwater that has not passed through any mechanical systems. Like the liquid in the womb, which is natural and pure, a divine creation without any human intervention, the *mikve*, as well, contains natural water, as given to us by the Creator.

Most *mikva'ot* today are clean and well cared for, and no less hygienic than the swimming pool on your kibbutz. There as well, dozens, hundreds, of people splash around, but you still enjoy bathing there. Fortunately for us, modern methods of disinfection allow us today to immerse in clean *mikva'ot*, in which even physicians – male and female – would not hesitate to immerse.

In any event, when I go to the *mikve* every year on the day before Yom Kippur, I really feel purified, like a new man who is starting off a new year with a clean slate. Obviously, the *mikve* is a part of a complete system of rituals and prayers that reinforce this feeling on Yom Kippur. I likewise imagine that a woman who immerses experiences that feeling of renewal that is so important precisely in married life.

Tomorrow, I'm supposed to go home, and on the way, I hope to pass a lovely spring in this area and to immerse there in preparation for Pesach. I hope to hear from you about the seminar right after Pesach.

In the meantime, I wish you a happy and kosher Pesach,

Dov

APRIL 9, 1972

Dear Dov,

It's a pity, a real pity that you weren't at the Pesach seminar. It was simply amazing! This time, we weren't at Kfar Etzion but at a new town called Alon Shvut, about a kilometer from Kfar Etzion. We stayed in small prefab homes used to house the students of the yeshiva, which has moved from Kfar Etzion to Alon Shvut. I finally met Hagi. I signed up for his discussion group, in which we learned the first chapter of Rabbi Yehuda HaLevi's *Kuzari*. You certainly must know that book.

Our topic was "The Exodus from Egypt and Its Meaning for Future Generations" (a topic chosen due to Pesach). I understood for the first time that Jewish belief is not something old-fashioned or primitive. Rabbi Yehuda HaLevi's words are really convincing. Maya,[1] my friend who came with me to the seminar, has already gone to Haifa and bought the *Kuzari* with a translation in modern Hebrew by Rabbi Genizi, and we decided that we would try to learn it together. I'm rather skeptical about whether we will be able to do it without someone's guidance. Maybe we'll ask our Bible teacher to help us. Maya suggested we invite you and Hagi to give a talk to our whole class at the kibbutz. That could be very interesting. Are you game?

I really envy you that you were on the Golan Heights. I love hiking there more than anywhere else in Israel. The brooks, springs, and waterfalls there are enchanting. We've gone several times to visit Merom Golan and Ein Zivan.[2] Several members of our kibbutz are among the founders of the Golan Heights communities, and they are always trying to attract more young people to live there. I actually am leaning more toward doing a year of Sherut Leumi (National Service) in a development town before the army. That attracts me more than going to the new kibbutzim on the Golan Heights or the Jordan Valley. In the development towns, you work with people who I think are in great need of help and support, more important than picking apples in the Heights or tomatoes in the valley.

Awaiting your response,

Talia

ב"ה

2 Iyar 5732 [April 16, 1972]

Dear Talia,

I was happy to read in your letter that the Pesach seminar was successful. The *Kuzari* is without a doubt a basic book of Jewish philosophy, and I too was very influenced by it. His arguments

---

[1] Not her real name; a pseudonym was used to protect her privacy.

[2] A kibbutz in the northern Golan Heights.

are simple and logical, and I agree with you that it is hard not
to be convinced. I'm not sure that your Bible teacher is the best
address to guide you in studying that book. From your letters, I
got the impression that for him there is only the Bible, according to scientific research and biblical criticism, and all the rest
– Midrash, Talmud, and traditional commentaries – is a sort of
worthless, insignificant addition.

Look, Talia, for me there is one complete Judaism, which
includes the Written Torah and the Oral Torah. For me, the
Bible and the Midrash, Jewish law and homiletics, philosophy
and Kabbala, are like the different floors in a tall building, with
one built upon the next. I believe that this entire large edifice
draws its inspiration from the divine Revelation at Mount
Sinai. Whoever tries to remove one floor from that edifice will
ultimately cause the entire building to collapse. Although you
wrote me that on your kibbutz you learn a lot of Bible, I am convinced that the next generation of secular education will scorn
even the Bible, because the Bible without our sages' input, and
without the tradition of all the generations, is a valueless thing
that cannot survive.

I suggest that you ask your Bible teacher where he studied
as a child, and I would guess that he will answer you that he
learned in a *heder*[1] or a yeshiva. From there he imbibed his love
of Scripture, but there, the Bible was part of an entire culture.
Today, he teaches the Bible as a book of ancient myths, and I am
certain that he will not succeed, using that approach, in imbu-
ing his students with a love of the Bible. The fact is that you
yourself wrote me that you don't like his classes, even though
my impression is that you greatly admire his knowledge.

I talked with Hagi about your suggestion, and he happily
agreed to come to the kibbutz for a talk with your class. He told
me that he was very impressed by you and by Maya as serious girls who think deeply. He has a booklet of talks by Rabbi
Tzvi Yehuda Kook about the *Kuzari* (he learned the book with
Rabbi Tzvi Yehuda as a study partner). He thinks the booklet

---

[1] A Jewish elementary school.

could help you to advance in your study of this important work. Anyway, I'm curious to hear your Bible teacher's answer to the question. I assume he may be unwilling to admit where he learned.

Take care,

Dov

APRIL 25, 1972

Dear Dov,

You were right. You were so right!

First of all, my Bible teacher really is a yeshiva graduate. He studied in a yeshiva in Lithuania and came to Israel before the Holocaust. Here he joined the preparatory group that established our kibbutz, and after several years of work as a farmer, he went to study Bible at the Kibbutz Seminar for Teachers in Oranim.

But the main thing you were right about was regarding his reaction to the *Kuzari*. We came to him, Maya and me, and we asked him for guidance in studying Rabbi Yehuda HaLevi's book. For a moment he seemed in shock, and he asked where we had heard about the book. We told him that we were at the Gesher seminar during Pesach and had learned the first chapter of the book. We told him that we were very impressed by the arguments used by Rabbi Yehuda HaLevi, and that we wanted to continue studying it. He got really angry at us and claimed that the whole book is full of unscientific, unsubstantiated mysticism. He got so angry that we thought he was going to suffer a heart attack any moment!

The next evening, he invited us to his home, and this time he was a lot calmer. He asked us to explain to him what we liked about the *Kuzari*. We told him that the main point that convinced us was the author's distinguishing between Judaism on the one hand, and Christianity and Islam on the other. Judaism is based on Mount Sinai, where God revealed Himself to the entire Jewish people, who in every generation handed down the story of what happened there. By contrast, Christianity and Islam are based on reputed revelations to solitary individuals, who reported them to their disciples, with the stories passing on from them to the public at large.

We told him that a revelation that took place in the presence of an entire people cannot be a bluff or the invention of a single individual. Such a story has credibility and is very convincing. (Do you think I understood the *Kuzari* right? If I am mistaken, please correct me.)

He was quiet for a long time, and then he said that Rabbi Yehuda HaLevi was right about Christianity and Islam, that no credibility or scientific value should be ascribed to their stories. Yet he was mistaken about Judaism, since according to the science of biblical criticism, the Torah's stories were written many generations after the Exodus. The tradition about what happened at the Exodus was transmitted orally, and it is therefore natural that it changed and was blown out of proportion, and we cannot know scientifically what is the true historic essence and what constitutes the embellishments added on through the generations. He actually begged us to stop studying nonscientific books from the Middle Ages, a time when science had not yet developed, insisting that all the theories that cropped up then have long since been disproved. He suggested that after school hours we organize a biblical criticism club in which he would explain to us in detail how scientific Biblical research came to its conclusions.

In the end, he said something that got me angry. He told us that he had approached the education committee, asking that they not authorize student participation in the Gesher seminars, since students come back from them very confused. Who is he to tell us where to go?! The truth is, however, that we are now very confused. Maya asked me to pressure Hagi to come to our kibbutz, and maybe we could hold a public debate between him and our teacher. I apologize for this confused letter.

Signed: The Confused One, Talia

ב"ה

20 Iyar 5732 [May 4, 1972]

Dear Talia,

I spoke with Hagi and he happily agreed to come to your kibbutz for a talk. He also has no problem with your teacher participating in the talk. I too think that this will only add to the discussion and make it deeper. According to your letters, he is a very erudite and interesting person. I suggest that we come on May 17, which is before Shavuot, the holiday of the giving of the Torah. That is really an appropriate time to talk about topics of faith and tradition.

I agree with your teacher that biblical criticism puts in question the reliability of the story that appears in the Torah. Without a doubt, whoever argues that the stories in the Torah about the Exodus and the Sinai Revelation were not written when they occurred, but hundreds of years afterwards, ascribes to those stories much less historic and scientific value. All the same, even if we accept the assumptions of biblical criticism (and I don't accept a word of it), one cannot entirely reject the arguments of Rabbi Yehuda HaLevi. It is an irrefutable fact that only Judaism has dared to claim that an entire people was present at the revelation of its religion's inauguration. It is a fact that neither Christianity, nor Islam, nor other religions – in fact, no other religion in the history of human culture (you can read about that in the Encyclopedia of Religions, published by Ofakim) – has claimed that an entire people, or even a large population, was present at its original revelation. All the other religions base their beliefs on a story concerning a supposed revelation to an individual, who then reported it to his disciples and followers. That's how all the religions began. Judaism is the only religion that has dared to make a claim of a revelation to a public, to an entire people, who not only were present at the historic occasion, but who experienced themselves – from the greatest of them to the most simple maidservant – an experience of divine revelation. An entire people that heard the voice of God talking to them – the Ten Commandments – and told about it with excitement, generation after generation, year after year.

Why didn't Christianity or Islam dare to make up a similar story about the start of the Christian or Islamic faith? Because it is impossible to lie when you are talking about a mass event; because regarding an entire people, it is impossible to report things that never happened, things that would cause listeners to fall on the floor laughing. Now the story of the Jewish people during the Exodus and the Sinai Revelation not only did not cause the Jews to fall on the floor laughing (after all, we tell this story every year at the Pesach Seder), but other nations as well ultimately accepted this story. After all, Christianity accepted the Bible and is based on it (they call the Hebrew Bible the Old Testament). The Koran, as well, relates in great detail the story of Israel's Exodus from the land of Egypt and the story of the Sinai Revelation. It's hard to believe that a story that was accepted by three widespread faiths, encompassing billions of believers throughout the world, is just some bluff or imaginary invention by someone, however smart he might be. It has to be something true and verified.

I hope we will meet soon and then we will be able to continue talking about this. Anyway, I have prepared you a small gift in preparation for our meeting (which I hope will be soon) – a thematically organized selection from the *Kuzari*. This is a very useful book compiled by one of the important rabbis of the ultra-Orthodox community, Rabbi Yehezkel Sarna, one of the heads of the Hebron Yeshiva in Jerusalem.

Until we meet,

Dov

MAY 9, 1972

Dear Dov,

Today I received your letter and I am answering it the same day. I spoke with my homeroom teacher and she agreed for you to come – you and Hagi – for a meeting with our class on Wednesday, May 17, at 12:30 p.m. In your honor, the last two classes of that day are being canceled (what luck that it fell out on math classes...). Our Bible teacher will also take part, and, obviously, our homeroom teacher. She suggested that the meeting should be a little bit more personal, that you should talk about yourselves, and about the yeshiva experience, and less philosophy...

Just this moment, they announced on the radio that the army has liberated the captives from the Sabena jet.[1] What an explosion of joy there was in our classroom! Everybody hugged and kissed. I was so happy I literally jumped up to the ceiling. I am so proud of our country, a small country of less than three million citizens, which does not surrender to terror and knows how to fight and to defend itself. Even large countries admire us. Now the American president[2] is talking on the radio, blessing Israel over the operation's success. Think for a moment, Dov, about what a special country we live in. The head of the world's greatest superpower, the president of the United States, blessing and praising a tiny country that is fighting bravely against the entire Arab and Muslim world...

All evening we talked about Guy, who is a soldier in the unit that freed captives. When Guy comes home to the kibbutz on leave, he never says a word about what he does in the army,

---

[1] The day before, on May 8, 1972, a Belgian Sabena jet was hijacked by four terrorists. The hijackers forced the pilots to land at Israel's Lod Airport and demanded the release of hundreds of imprisoned terrorists in exchange for the release of the captives, mostly Israelis. The Israeli government, headed by Prime Minister Golda Meir, rejected the terrorists' demands out of hand. The next day, elite Israeli troops (under the command of Ehud Barak, and with Binyamin Netanyahu participating) stormed the hijacked jet and freed the passengers. Two terrorists were killed in the operation and two were captured.

[2] Richard Nixon.

but everyone knows that he is in an elite unit that carries out a lot of special operations. Today, the whole kibbutz was proud that Guy participated in this marvelous operation. It would be great if every day could be as joyous as this one!

Maya and I are waiting impatiently for you. It feels so strange that we've been writing for more than half a year already and I've never seen you in person. I hope you come and don't disappoint us.

Very happily yours,

Talia

May 21, 1972

Dear Dov,

First of all, I would like to thank you and Hagi for taking the trouble to come to our school. I know this was a whole-day affair for you, but I think your effort was worth it. From my point of view, the meeting was very successful, although there were some who were disappointed and even angry. The fact is, instead of the hour and a half set aside for the meeting, almost half the class stayed with you for more than three hours. For most of the kids, this was their first encounter with religious people, and for most of them it was interesting and even fascinating. The personal story of Hagi, who was born on a secular kibbutz and became religious, was really a surprise for me. When I met him at the Gesher seminar on Pesach, it never occurred to me that he could have ever been secular. He acts and talks like all the religious people who grew up in religious families.

Today, in Bible class, our teacher related to the things Hagi said. He argued that Hagi avoided all the questions about biblical criticism, and instead of talking about the Bible from a scientific perspective, he talked about general things, about Jewish history and Zionism. He thought that was entirely irrelevant to the central question about whether the Bible stories are historic fact or imaginative legends without a scientific basis. He actually preferred what you had to say, because he thought it was obvious that Hagi wants to turn the whole class religious, but you were just telling about your spiritual world and about your way of life.

Maya is very enthusiastic about Hagi and says he is very convincing, and her parents are really afraid she's going to become religious. I was pleased to meet you and really liked what you had to say. I haven't decided yet if I support my Bible teacher's opinion or Hagi's, but what you said was very personal and interesting. It's a shame the meeting went on so long and in the end you hurried to the bus, and there was no time left for us to talk personally. I wanted to get to know you a little better. But I hope that will happen next time. Maya and I are already planning your next meeting with our class, maybe not the whole class but at least those that took an interest and asked questions. I hope our homeroom teacher will let us invite you to another meeting.

Thanks for coming, Dov. Regards to Hagi (let me remind you that are you not allowed to show him the letters).

Sincerely,

Talia

P.S. Thanks for the book you brought me. I have already started to read it.

ב"ה

20 Sivan 5732 [June 2, 1972]

Dear Talia,

I too was very excited by my visit to your kibbutz. Hagi came from the secular world, but for me this was my first time meeting a class in a secular school. I was really surprised by the enormous interest and by the level of the questions. I felt like this meeting filled a huge gap that exists for you because you don't have religious teachers. I understood that for most of the students in your class, the meeting with us was their first meeting with religious people. It's a shame there aren't more meetings like this. When all is said and done, we are one people with a shared fate and common enemies.

I think Hagi did not at all avoid the questions about biblical criticism. He said explicitly that he does not wish in this meeting to deal with biblical criticism (although he has a lot to say about that subject), because he wanted to explain why he accepts Jewish belief even if all the claims of biblical criticism are correct. From the standpoint of the argument he presented, it doesn't matter whether Deuteronomy was written in Moses' day 3,400 years ago (as Jewish tradition claims), or in Josiah's day at the end of the First Temple period, 2,700 years ago (as biblical criticism argues). In any event, we are talking about a book written thousands of years ago, dozens of generations ago. And here you have a book that prophesies precisely the entire process of Jewish history, including what is happening in our day.

In my ears, there still echoes the silence that fell upon the room when Hagi read chapter 28 of Deuteronomy and showed that everything written there was fulfilled over the two thousand years of exile of the Jewish people, down to the last detail. And even more stark was the silence when Hagi read chapter 30, verse by verse, and showed how all the prophecies there are being fulfilled in our day with the return to Zion: the ingathering of the exiles (there is almost no nation on earth from which immigrants have not come to Israel), the flowering of the land, desolate for two thousand years (Israel is one of the world's leading nations today in the realm of agriculture, and our fruits – with "Jaffa" stamped on them – are world famous), and the wars, and the victories over all our enemies (despite our being a tiny country, we have beaten the Arab countries in three wars within twenty years – the War of Independence, the Sinai Campaign, and the Jerusalem War, called the Six-Day War).

Talia, think about what an amazing thing is happening before our eyes: no nation exiled from its land thousands of years ago has maintained its identity or survived. All of them assimilated and were swallowed up within large, strong nations, which themselves disintegrated and were swallowed up within new empires. Where are the Ammonites and the Moabites, the Egyptians and the Syrians, the Babylonians and the Persians, the Greeks and the Romans...? All of them disappeared and from

During army service in the Golan Heights, where he met Talia's father, 1971

their cultures only archaeological traces remain, sitting in museums the world over. Yet tiny Israel, which was exiled thousands of years ago and dispersed to the four corners of the earth, lives and endures! It preserved its identity, culture, faith and language, its affinity for its ancient homeland, and after thousands of years was privileged to return to that homeland, to make the desert bloom, to defeat enemies far more numerous, and to establish anew its independent country. Is that not enough reason for us to believe that there is something divine in this people, that transcends all the natural powers of the rest of the nations?

The amazing thing is that this whole process, unparalleled in human history, is described in an exceedingly detailed manner in the Bible and in our sages' expositions. Is that something human, that somebody should stand up thousands of years ago (and it doesn't matter if it was 2,700 years ago or 3,400 years ago) and should foresee the entire unique, convoluted history of the Jewish people thousands of years into the future? I am convinced that no human being, no matter how wise, how extraordinary, could foresee such a complex and unique process thousands of years into the future – and that his whole forecast would be fulfilled, detail after detail, stage after stage, completely and precisely. It is a fact that besides the Bible, no book in human history has foreseen any historic process, even one much shorter and less complex. Does that not transform the Bible into a divine work?

For me, the answer to this question is very clear, and it transforms my faith into something that is not only emotional and mystical but very intellectual and rational. The fact that I spoke more about my life in yeshiva and Hagi spoke more about the philosophical side of faith is due to our having divided up the work between us. Hagi arrived at faith after many years of reading and research and much struggle, and the topic of consolidating one's faith intellectually really burns within him. But believe me, Talia, that I too would very much like to see you and Maya and all the secular Jews come closer to Judaism – both within the realm of faith and in the practical realm of mitzva observance.

By the way, on the bus, as we were returning to the yeshiva from the kibbutz, Hagi told me that he learned this approach, of reaching faith by considering Jewish history as the fulfillment of the divine promise to the Jewish people, from Rabbi Tzvi Yehuda Kook, the head of the Mercaz HaRav Yeshiva. He told me that this past year he was privileged to have Rabbi Kook as a personal study partner, and that really built up his faith.

We will be happy to come back for another meeting even if it involves a smaller group. Send regards to all the kids in your class, who made the conversation so pleasant and friendly. Thanks also to your homeroom teacher. For me as well, the meeting was too short, and very exciting. We will try to complete the discussion next time.

Sincerely,

Dov

JUNE 10, 1972

Dear Dov,

The meeting with you is continuing to stir up the class. In history class, several students raised the issue of faith based on Jewish history. There was a very stormy discussion, which went on into the next class. Our history teacher argued that the Bible really does explain Jewish history, but not like Hagi and you believe. In her view, the Bible is not a divine prophecy that has been fulfilled, but a human prophecy that fulfilled itself due to its moral strength. She read to us the vision of the end of days from Isaiah, which charges the Jewish people with a moral mission of instilling brotherhood and peace among all mankind: "And they shall beat their swords into plowshares, and their spears into pruning hooks. Nation shall not take up sword against nation. They shall never again know war" [Isaiah 2:4]. (She asked us to copy these verses into our notebooks, and I took it from there.) This vision is so great and important that it gave the Jews the strength to endure, in order to fulfill it. It wasn't God, but that moral vision, which gave the Jewish people the strength to survive. For that reason, she very much supports Bible study, especially the Prophets, because in her view that is what will give the State of Israel, as well, the strength to survive, and without the Bible, we have no chance of surviving as a Jewish state. (She is a Bible teacher in the kibbutz elementary school.)

When she was talking, I remembered our class trip from a year ago. We were at Kibbutz Sdei Boker, and we met with Ben-Gurion. It's already been several years since he was the prime minister, so he has more time to meet with students. He too spoke with us a lot about the Bible, and about the moral vision of the prophet Isaiah. I remember that at the end of his talk, he repeated several times (each time raising his voice even more) that without the Bible, our country cannot endure. At the time, I didn't take such pronouncements so seriously, but today I think I understand this idea, and even identify with it to a certain extent. (All the same, I'm after two Gesher seminars and almost a year of writing you.)

Dov, what do you think about what the history teacher said? A lot of kids said that it's very logical and understandable, more than your and Hagi's religious explanation.

Our homeroom teacher agreed to our having another meeting with you, but since summer vacation is approaching, she suggested that the meeting be held after the vacation just before Rosh Hashana and Yom Kippur. Since that is several months away, I suggest, Dov, that we meet, you and I, during the break. This can give us a good chance to get to know each other better, and not just with philosophical discussions.

Looking forward to your answer,

Talia

❖ ❖ ❖

ב"ה

7 TAMMUZ 5732 [JUNE 19, 1972]

Dear Talia,

I am happy that the meeting with your class is still making waves. That's a sign that we succeeded in making you think, and also that we apparently gave you enough food for thought. I, obviously, do not entirely agree with your history teacher. I don't think that the amazing, unique phenomena of Jewish history can be explained in human terms. Think about it. If these phenomena were influenced solely by human factors, then they would have had to occur in other nations or cultures as well; and even if not to the same extent, then at least in a similar way. Every historical development repeats itself, and some kind of cyclic law has to apply to it. Yet here it turns out that the history of the Jewish people is so different from anything else, so unique and anomalous, that no other nation's experience even comes close to it.

What people survived for thousands of years in such a difficult exile and preserved their identity like the Jewish people? What lands remained loyal to the people that left it thousands of years ago, remaining parched and desolate, and only when that people returned from their exile did the land once more flourish and prosper like the land of Israel? What book succeeded in sketching in precise, detailed lines, a people's history over thousands of years like the Bible? In short, nothing we know of human civilization, in which there are thousands of nations, religions, and cultures, reminds us even slightly of the Jewish people, the land of Israel, and our book of books, the Bible. For me, the meaning of this is that we are talking about a divine and not a human phenomenon.

Hagi once gave me a little book called *BiShvilei Emunat Yisrael* [Pathways to Jewish faith] by Dr. Yehoshua Yevin, a physician and historian who was one of the founders of the pre-state Lehi underground group.[1] There I found a very interesting sentence that describes precisely my reaction to your history teacher's comments. Dr. Yevin writes that a vision so great, a vision that succeeded in sustaining an entire nation under such difficult conditions like those faced by the Jewish people for thousands of years, is one that has to contain in it something divine.

Consider, Talia, how Soviet Russia looks. They had a great vision – a just, egalitarian society that worried about every individual. What became of that great vision? A horribly cruel, corrupt country. (Recently I read Solzhenitsyn's book *Cancer Ward*. Shocking.) Only now are the dimensions of Stalin's slaughter of his people starting to become clear. Some talk of sixty million people that he murdered. Do you know why

---

[1] Lehi (Lohamei Herut Israel, "Fighters for the Freedom of Israel," also known as the Stern Group for its leader, Avraham Stern) was a small, radical split-off group from the main dissident Jewish defense group, Etzel (Irgun Tzvai Leumi, "National Military Organization"). Formed in 1940 with a policy of armed struggle against the colonizing British forces in Mandate Palestine, Lehi pushed for the formation of the State of Israel and fought together with the other Jewish defense organizations in the 1948 War of Independence against the Arabs.

this happened? Because the communists rid their culture and their educational system of God and the Bible, and closed all the synagogues, churches, and mosques.

Without God, people are left empty, and within that emptiness, all their evil drives burst forth, the beast within man. In short, a great vision does not guarantee a thing. It was the Jewish people who succeeded in establishing exemplary communities, communities that became famous for their charity, love of man, solidarity, and mutual sense of responsibility. And all that despite the terrible conditions of a people in exile, pursued, smitten, and humiliated.

Do you know why? It's because God was there. Where there is God, there is holiness, there is love, there are values, there is true culture. I hope you are not insulted, but you asked, and I promised that we would be sincere and frank. So I'm really acting that way.

Talia, I want to be open with you about something else. I'm sorry to disappoint you, but I've decided that we can't meet personally at present. I went to my rabbi for advice on this, and he too supported my decision. I'm already twenty-one years old (my birthday was a month ago, May 16), and at my age I'm looking for a friend for life, a woman with whom I hope to build my home. I believe that at this age all my energy has to be directed toward that goal, and not to various types of friendships not directed toward establishing a family. Obviously, I will be happy to come to you at your kibbutz, but only in the framework of a talk with your class or a lecture to the kibbutz members. My rabbi suggested that I shouldn't even go to a talk or lecture alone, but with Hagi or another boy from my yeshiva. Obviously, I will be happy for us to keep writing. My correspondence with you gives me a lot of food for thought and provides me with a real challenge.

Hoping you'll keep on writing,

Dov

JUNE 28, 1972

Dear Dov,

First of all, *mazel tov* (a bit late) on your birthday. It's nice you remembered to tell me. This time I had a hard time with your letter. I'm disappointed that you're not willing to meet me outside the framework of meetings with my class. I just don't get it. At our age, why is there no room for friendship between boys and girls not directed toward marriage? What, we can't be friends? Is contact between boys and girls limited to looking for a wedding candidate? You've got to explain yourself a bit more on this point, although I don't believe I'll succeed in changing your approach.

Instead of my meeting with you, I organized with Maya a meeting with two religious girls from Haifa who were with us at the Gesher seminar during Pesach. We were in the same room, and it will be nice to keep up the contact that started at the seminar.

I was also very insulted by your declarations that without faith in God there are no values and no morality. What? In our kibbutz there are no values? Look at how people on our kibbutz forgo the good salaries they could be earning if they lived in the city, and instead they work for the sake of our quality of life as a community, with the values of cooperation. That's not values? Look how on our kibbutz they care for the elderly members, unhesitatingly supporting families with handicapped children, and all at the expense of the work performed by members. That's not values? A lot of young people go off for a year of National Service before the army (and not at the expense of their army time) to new kibbutzim on the Golan Heights and the Jordan Valley, or to the development towns in the Negev. That's not values? I don't understand why you associate morality with religion or religious faith in the first place. Morality depends on the education a person receives, the social environment he grew up in, and, obviously, his own character and personality. In my opinion, there's no connection between religion and social values. In short, I had a hard time with your letter and now you owe me explanations.

Looking forward to your response,

Talia

ב"ה

28 Tammuz 5732 [July 10, 1972]

Dear Talia,

I well understand that you were insulted by my last letter, and I also understand why. Even so, I'm not going to change my outlook, that there is a deep connection between morality and faith in God. You justifiably ask whether there are no values on the kibbutz where you live. Sure there are. I think the kibbutz is a very idealistic society with a high moral level. As far as that goes, you are really preaching to the converted. But...(and this is a big "but") this ethical state will not last long if the kibbutz does not add a religious dimension to its worldview and way of life.

Look, Talia, all (or almost all) of the founders of the kibbutzim came from religious families. They studied Torah when they were young, and they absorbed faith in their childhood. And even after they became secular, their moral values (and, one might add, their nationalist values as well) that they had grown up with remained imprinted upon them. Yet already the second generation, who grew up on secular kibbutzim and did not soak up the atmosphere of the traditional Jewish community, are less idealistic and more materialistic than their parents. You yourself told me that today on the kibbutz, the chief topic at membership meetings is how to decide who gets to go abroad first.

The third generation (you and your friends), who grew up with less attachment to Judaism and the Bible than the second generation, will, I think, be more materialistic than the second generation. I will risk a prophecy (which, as is known, was granted only to fools) that in the next generation, most of the kibbutzniks will grow tired of the cooperative spirit and all the ideals associated with it, and will want to develop their personal careers and earn as much money as possible. Possibly, the entire kibbutz structure will collapse, since the ideals at the core of the kibbutz require an affinity for religious faith. Without it, those ideals will give way to egocentrism (where the individual and not the community is at the center) and the sense of mutual responsibility and egalitarianism will make way for the worship of money.[1]

Look, in order to concede and sacrifice in the material realm for the sake of values and ideals, you've got to believe that there are absolute values worth conceding and sacrificing for. I think a person without faith in God, Who constitutes a source of absolute truth and eternal values, will have a hard time consciously consolidating, and even more so emotionally internalizing, the existence of absolute values. Ultimately, without a belief in something supreme and absolute, transcending finite, limited man, every value can be questioned and debated. In a world of moral uncertainty, only one thing remains concrete: one's ego, operating on behalf of one's private interests and the material pleasures of the moment.

This description probably sounds to you extreme and exaggerated, and you are absolutely right. After all, the Torah testifies that man was created "in the image of God." He thus has a moral conscience stamped within him, and it is very hard for him to shake it off. At the same time, however, it is an image *of God*, and the more a person distances himself from God in his faith, worldview, and way of life, the more the divine image within him is weakened, until it fades away entirely. The "image of God" stamped upon man, from which derives our

---

[1] Less than forty years after Dov wrote these words, the Israeli newspaper *Haaretz* reported, "Only a quarter of kibbutzim still function as equalized cooperatives, while the rest have begun paying salaries to their members." Eli Ashkenazi, "After 100 Years, the Kibbutz Movement Has Completely Changed," *Haaretz*, January 7, 2010.

natural propensity for morality, needs to be strengthened and nourished, buttressed and developed. A person needs both to strengthen his faith in God, and to strengthen his moral sensitivity. The Torah says, "Love your neighbor as yourself. I am the Lord" (Leviticus 19:18), to emphasize that without "I am the Lord," "Love your neighbor as yourself" cannot long endure.

In general, the Bible always links faith to morality, but secular Israeli society has removed the religious dimension and tried to build a moral ideology without God. The Bible says, "Walk modestly with your God" (Micah 6:8), but the Hebrew Reali School of Haifa[2] took as its logo only the words "Walk modestly." The Torah says that man was created "in the image of God," but in modern Hebrew we have gotten used to saying that man was "created in the image." (In the American Constitution, which bases human dignity on faith in God, the full term appears: "in the image of God.")

I do not believe that the attempt to build a moral society without God will succeed. We saw what the "moral atheism" of Soviet Russian Communism led to.

By now I'm really tired, and my head hurts from writing so much. You must certainly have sensed that what I wrote in this letter, I wrote with a stormy spirit. I have literally hit upon the deepest point of my worldview, a point that defines my life, and that I think about daily. It's hard for me to write any more, but I hope you won't be insulted, because precisely the closeness that has developed between us has enabled me to share with you my deepest thoughts. And precisely the great appreciation I have of you forces me to be open with you, and not to write things I don't believe.

---

[2] Founded in 1913 in Haifa before the outbreak of World War I, the Hebrew Reali School is one of the oldest private schools in Israel, whose educational philosophy promotes the values of Zionism, humanism, tolerance, and democracy. Among its thousands of alumni are prominent members in Israeli society, including one former Israeli president, three chiefs of General Staff of the Israel Defense Forces, and four Supreme Court justices.

As far as a personal meeting between us, I'll write about that in my next letter, because I want to think about that again, and to get advice once more from my rabbi.

In any event, I hope that for now we will continue writing even if we don't meet, because I feel that the need to deal with your questions is really developing and crystallizing my worldview. I hope our correspondence is helping you, as well, to develop. For me it adds a lot, and for that I thank you.

Take care,

Dov

JULY 16, 1972

Dear Dov,

Instead of meeting with you, Maya and I met with two religious girls, Naomi and Tamar, who were with us on the last Gesher seminar. We walked around for quite a long time looking for a kosher place where we could sit. I never thought it would be so hard to find a kosher place in Haifa. Everywhere we tried they said they're kosher but open on Shabbat. But Naomi and Tamar insisted we should sit only in a place with a *kashrut* certificate. In the end, we found a pretty nice place, but it was crowded, because all the religious Jews come there on Saturday night.

We talked a lot about your last letter, and they, too, agreed that there doesn't have to be a connection between morality and faith in God. They, too, think that a normal person behaves ethically because he wants to live in a society that has a good quality of life and good human relations. If he steals or cheats, then everyone will do the same thing, and society will very quickly turn into hell. By contrast, if he helps others, they, too, will help him when he needs it. So where is God in this story?

They were very surprised to hear that you are uncertain whether to meet me personally. They told me that they have a friend whose father is a rabbi, who has been going out for several months with a secular boy from the neighborhood. So maybe, all the same, you've got second thoughts on this? And anyway, why can't a religious person and a secular person marry each other and live a good, happy life together? If there is true love, I think it's possible to overcome all the differences, showing consideration and respect for the one you love.

In short, we had a fun time together until almost midnight (because we don't have to get up for school – we're on vacation!). We barely caught the last bus back to our kibbutz, which leaves at exactly midnight. All in all, even the religious are nice people who like to have a good time, and for me that is the big discovery of the year. I always thought that the religious just spend all day praying in synagogue and studying Torah in yeshiva. I've discovered some really great religious people. But you seem more serious to me, because you really do study and read books all day, and you go to ask your rabbi about every little thing. Even so, your letters are very interesting, and I hope you will continue to write. I understand that you, too, will soon have vacation from yeshiva, so please write more.

Take care,

Talia

❖ ❖ ❖

ב"ה

12 MENAHEM AV 5732 [JULY 23, 1972]

Dear Talia,

I was happy to hear from you that you are continuing your social connections with the religious girls you met at the seminar. I believe you'll be able to learn as much about Judaism from that as from my letters. What you learn in a conversation is worth a lot more than what you read in a book or a letter.

Right now you are for sure asking yourself: So why doesn't Dov agree to meet with me and to talk with me face-to-face? It's because I don't agree with you. I don't think it's desirable for a religious person to marry an irreligious person. I know that sounds unfair to you, because after all, we are all Jews. That is true, but we also know how different are the spiritual worlds and the daily way of life of a religious Jew and a secular Jew. Married life involves a lot of difficulties and crises as it is. Between a husband and wife, even when their spiritual and cultural worlds are similar, there are many innate differences, warranting a lot of strength of character for the couple to bond and cohere. Why add the big differences that exist between a religious person and a secular person?

Think for a moment about Shabbat in such a family: one spouse wants to go to the beach, visit his parents, or just go out. The other insists on staying home, going to synagogue, hearing a rabbi's Torah lecture, or, at most, spending some time in the nearby playground. Think about how much tension there can be every Shabbat when these differences arise. Why add unnecessary tension to the frictions that exist anyway in every normal family?

Think also about the family life of such a couple. Suppose one spouse wants to keep the family purity laws (you should already know what that is), and the other spouse views it as just an old-fashioned, primitive custom. Think about how much tension can be created on this background. After all, the issue is not something petty, but a supreme effort of restraint and self-control, which has a chance only when you believe and identify with the faith and worldview that stand behind the religious way of life.

You are for sure saying to yourself now: Dov doesn't understand what love is. Seemingly, when there is true love, one can overcome all the difficulties and crises.

That is true but that is also not true. It's true that love is a necessary condition for a happy married life, and without it, nothing can last. Yet I don't think it is a sufficient condition. After all, physical attraction erodes over the years, and in its place come a lot of pressures and tensions. If there is no shared spiritual world out of which the couple can draw on shared values and psychic resources to continue nurturing the marital bond, there is no chance the bond will last.

Talia, I sometimes imagine how hard it must be to keep the family purity laws. After all, you're talking about a married couple who sleep together in the same room (albeit in separate beds) and love each other. You're not talking about a onetime thing, but about two weeks of living like a monk each month. I picture to myself that there are a lot of moments of harsh struggle, of great pain, of biting one's lip. In those difficult moments, I want my wife to strengthen and encourage me, and to whisper to me not only words of love but, chiefly, words of faith in God, of becoming stronger in undertaking the yoke of heaven. Otherwise, who knows if I won't stumble or fail, God forbid. After all, you know from my previous letters that I believe that ultimately the effort pays off and leads to a happier life even here on this earth, and not just in the World to Come. But the pathway to happiness involves hard work, based on great faith.

Talia, as long as you don't feel you can share this great faith in a Creator of the Universe and in the Sinai Revelation, there is no room for a personal connection between us. After all, such a connection can develop (and we're not in total control of our emotions) and lead us both to decisions that will break our hearts. Why put ourselves through such a difficult trial? If our correspondence leads you to move closer to the world of faith and religion, we can weigh the possibility of a more personal bond between us. In the meantime, I suggest that we make do at present with writing, which is enriching me, and I hope it is enriching you too.

Just as in the realm of family, so too in other moral realms, I believe that a person needs great faith in the Creator of the Universe and in His Torah, which He gave us to overcome evil passions and selfish drives. Imagine a government functionary or bank manager discovering some breach in the system that enables him to steal millions of dollars without being caught (or at least with only a small risk). Consider what a great temptation he faces, for he has no fear of flesh and blood. At such moments, a person needs to feel that even when there is no police officer and no state comptroller, there is still "an eye that sees, and an ear that hears, and that all your deeds are inscribed in the ledger" (Tractate Avot, which deals with matters of morality and character). Yes, a person needs to recognize that he is "destined to give judgment before the supreme King of kings." It may be that no human being will catch him for his misdeeds, and he will not stand trial before any human court, but there is a court and there is a Judge "Whom nothing eludes" (from the High Holiday prayers).

You are probably saying to yourself: Look at Dov, who places no faith in man's good character and understanding. After all, man wants to lead a good life in a good society, in which there is no anarchy, crime, or corruption. So why does that desire not suffice? It turns out that it does not suffice. The fact is that we set up courthouses for criminals, and a large police force with detectives and investigators, and detailed laws with deterrent punishments, etc., etc. Yet even all that does not suffice, for man is limited, especially in understanding the thoughts and intentions of his fellow men.

Take, for example, the laws of bribery, about which we are unfortunately hearing more and more. According to Israeli criminal law, in order to convict a person for bribery, there has to be proven intent to benefit in exchange for the bribe. Yet we know how hard it is to prove intent, for in general, such transactions are carried out with a nod and a wink, or some innocuous expression. That is what makes it so hard to incriminate people in bribery trials.

Yet, if someone believes there is a Creator, and that He "examines what is in our heart," and knows our exact intentions, there is a greater chance that one will hold off and curb his strong impulse to take a bribe and to accept unlawful financial benefit.

Even faith in God is no guarantee. Even religious people, and even people who believe that God watches all of our actions, are liable to fall prey to sin. After all, man was given free will to choose between good and evil. Yet I have no doubt that a life with faith is a life with a bigger chance of vanquishing the evil impulse. A life with fear of God also means more fear of sin, which no human framework can create.

We should only be so fortunate, with God's help, to become stronger both in our fear of God and in our fear of sin.

Take care,

Dov

AUGUST 6, 1972

Dear Dov,

My letter was delayed because last week we were on a trip to the Sinai. This was my first time there, and I came home really excited about it. Everything there is so big – the enormous desert, which you travel through for hours, seeing nothing but unending yellow sand dunes; the humongous wadis, with frightening cliffs rising up hundreds of meters high on both sides (especially Wadi Piran); the tall mountains that literally reach the clouds (that's at Jebel Musa); and most of all, the breathtaking beaches with amazing coral reefs – the Eilat beaches pale by comparison (we went snorkeling both at Sharm el-Sheikh and at Dahab).

I thought about you when we were at the top of Moses' mountain, which the Arabs call Jebel Musa. According to Christian and Muslim tradition, it was there that Moses received the Torah, and it was from there that he brought the two tablets of the covenant down to the people of Israel. We spent several hours climbing up there at night, and we reached the top just moments before sunrise. The view was really breathtaking – mountaintops all around, shining with a reddish light, and between the mountains pathways of white fog and on the horizon the Suez Canal, lustrous and shining.

When we sat down to rest at the top, a stormy debate started up about whether the story about the giving of the

Torah at Sinai was real or just a legend. I was surprised that my friends had the strength to argue after four hours of fairly hard climbing. The most active in the debate was Maya, who actually quoted Rabbi Yehuda HaLevi from his *Kuzari* regarding the tradition and reliability of an event experienced by the masses, etc., etc. I think Maya is really going to become religious. When she talks, she already sounds like a believer. I didn't say anything, because I was pretty tired and I also felt very confused. I thought about you, because you for sure would have given us a lecture on the Bible or history, and everyone would have listened to you the way they listened when you talked to our class.

On the way home from the Sinai (which took us over ten hours), we argued about whether the Sinai should be returned to Egypt in exchange for a peace treaty. Most of the kids thought it simply doesn't make sense to give up the Sinai. They argued that twice already Egypt has broken agreements with us and blocked the Straits of Tiran to Israeli shipping.[1] What guarantee do we have that Egypt won't do it again if it controls Sinai? I actually suggested that perhaps it's worth trying, because the Egyptians have a new leader (Sadat) who may act differently than Nasser. It's true that Nasser was aggressive and hostile toward us, but Sadat makes a different impression. Maybe he will actually honor the agreements that he makes with us. In any event, I'm rather uncertain, and I would like to hear your views.

We came home so tired that we literally slept all Shabbat. Yet everybody was happy with the trip, and we are already planning another trip right after matriculation exams next summer.

I forgot to ask you if you've already been to the Sinai.

Awaiting your letter,

Talia

---

[1] The blockades took place in 1956, before the Sinai campaign, and in 1967, before the Six-Day War. In both instances, Egypt violated signed agreements with Israel, as well as international accords.

8 Elul 5732 [August 18, 1972]

Dear Talia,

How I envy you that you were privileged to climb Mount Sinai.
When I read your exciting letter, I suddenly heard the words of
the song, written during the Sinai campaign ("By Mount Sinai"
– Yehiel Mohar):

> It is no dream, my friend, it is no dream, my friend,
> No legend, if you will.
> Because at Mount Sinai,
> Because at Mount Sinai,
> The bush is burning
> Still.

I always get excited anew when I hear that song on the
radio. We've come back to Mount Sinai, where we received the
Torah thousands of years ago. And we haven't just returned to
it as tourists, but as a nation standing on its own two feet and
beating our enemies with a wonderful army and excellent soldiers. How exciting are the words that end the song:

> Now the holy flame burns
> In our hearts once more
> Tis the holy flame –
> As all the engines roar.
> The tale shall be told
> Of the return of the nation
> Back to the Sinai Revelation.

These words excite me, because they speak not only of the
return to Mount Sinai, but of the return to the Sinai Revelation.
They address not just the physical return to the expanses of the
land of Israel, but also the spiritual return that will follow.

Yes, Talia, Sinai is part of Eretz Yisrael, the land of Israel.
It is not the Eretz Yisrael that our ancestors lived in during the

biblical period, but it is still part of the land that God promised to give our ancestors at the end of days. God made this promise immediately after the Sinai Revelation: "I will set your borders from the Sea of Reeds to the Sea of Philistia" (Exodus 23:31). The Sea of Reeds hugs the Sinai from the south, from two directions, the Gulf of Sinai and the Gulf of Suez (it's a kind of love hug). Rabbi Yehuda HaLevi says the same thing in his *Kuzari*, when he describes the borders of the land of Israel.

I saw in one of the Torah commentaries (at this moment I don't remember which) that this is why God told Moses at the Sinai Revelation: "Remove your sandals from your feet, for the place in which you stand is holy ground" [Exodus 3:5]. After all, the burning bush episode was at Mount Sinai ("He came to Horeb, the mountain of God" [3:1]. The concept of "holy ground" is said only regarding Eretz Yisrael. Until the burning bush episode, Moses had been herding Jethro's sheep in Midian, which is outside the borders of the land of Israel, and now, for the first time in his life, he arrived within the land's borders. He was therefore commanded to remove his shoes in order to feel the holiness of the land.

You understand, Talia, that I relate to the debate that took place among you on your trip home from a totally different standpoint. My perspective is not political or security minded (i.e., whether Sadat will keep agreements or continue in the path of Nasser, who used to violate agreements), but, above all, a religious, faith-based perspective. God has now started to fulfill His promise to Israel, and He is returning us to the land. In the first stage, in the War of Independence, God returned us to part of Eretz Yisrael, and in the second stage, in the Six-Day War (which would better be called the War of Jerusalem's Liberation), He returned us to broader sections of it: to the expanses of Judea and Samaria, the Golan Heights and Sinai, and obviously, first and foremost, to Greater Jerusalem. Are we entitled to throw away this marvelous gift that He gave us in such a miraculous fashion? Within six days, we not only defeated the armies of Egypt, Jordan, and Syria, but we conquered parts of

Eretz Yisrael, sections six times larger than the State of Israel before the war.

A believing person embraces this marvelous gift with both arms, and transforms it into a catalyst of empowerment and of faith. At last, at last, the redemption of Israel is being fulfilled! At last, the divine promise is coming true! We have to use this marvelous gift to increase faith, to increase aliya, to increase settlement, to increase the joy of redemption, and not, God forbid, to spurn the great kindness done for us.

You know, Talia, that that great kindness did not end with the war. Only recently has the media reported that Israel discovered enormous oil fields in the Gulf of Suez in the area of Ras Sudr and Abu Rudeis. Is it a coincidence that when the Sinai was in the Egyptians' hands, oil was not discovered there, and when the Jewish people arrived in Sinai, suddenly the oil fields were discovered? For years we prayed that we should discover a bit of oil in our tiny land, and we were jealous of the Arab countries, which have enormous oil deposits. And now, this marvelous gift was given to us – oil fields, which apparently meet all the fuel needs of our country, even allowing us to export it. Finally, we can be an independent country economically, which stands on its own two feet and is not dependent on the kindness of other nations. Should we scorn this divine kindness, or use it to become stronger and to strengthen the redemption of Israel?

This question bothers me, since I fear that diplomatic or military or economic considerations do not suffice to tie us permanently to sections of our homeland liberated in war. When all is said and done, if a person believes that the Sinai is part of the land promised us by God, he will also be willing to give his life to fight for it. Yet if he lacks this inner awareness, if his starting point is not the Jewish people's deep affinity for all the expanses of the promised land (including the Gilead Mountains in Syria, and Lebanon, which are not yet in our hands) – then everything becomes relative, transient, I would almost say commercial (it then depends on what political or economic remuneration we receive in one transaction or another).

I was happy to hear from you that most of the kids hold that it is forbidden to give up Sinai and it is forbidden to be tempted by the promises of the Arabs, who until today have broken all of them. Yet I am still worried, since without a religious perspective, nothing, in my opinion, is strong and stable in the long term.

Eighth grade, at the Kotel (Western Wall). Right, *Dov;* left, *Haim Sabato.*

Rumor has it that the third portion of our military service, which we are supposed to begin in another half year, will be in the southern Sinai (the area of Sharm el-Sheikh and Santa Katarina). If, indeed, these rumors come true, I hope to be privileged like you to climb Mount Sinai, and like you, to go snorkeling on the marvelous Sinai beaches. Apart from one tank drill in the sands of Bir Temade, I haven't yet had the good fortune to be in Sinai, so I am really hoping that my third stretch of army duty will make up what is missing.

We are hoping to come to you for another talk before Rosh Hashana and Yom Kippur. You haven't yet given me a date or written what you expect from the second talk, or what topics we should focus on, so it will be a continuation of the first talk.

Last week, we returned to our yeshiva studies, so once more I am going to be limiting myself in my letters. It's late, and tomorrow I have to get up for a day of study and for morning prayers at six thirty (giving me barely three hours of sleep).

Take care,

Dov

SEPTEMBER 6, 1972

Dear Dov,

I am taking advantage of this long, tense night to answer your letter. We, too, started school again several days ago, and I took advantage of the last several days of vacation to make up all sorts of holes in math and English. And now this terrible night has befallen us. We've all stayed awake to follow what is happening with our sportsmen in Germany.[1] The radio is on, and every few minutes there is a report or an update from Germany, and everyone gets tense and listens and gets disappointed over and over that there is still no good news, no happy ending.

To break the terrible tension, I left the room for several minutes, and I am taking advantage of that to write you. Unfortunately, we won't be able to meet in the near future, because our teacher asked that our class's meeting with you and Hagi be postponed. She explained that the school year has just started, and the class has to get back into its routine following the summer break. She suggested that the meeting take place in

---

[1] On September 5, 1972, eleven Israeli sportsmen, who were participating in the Olympics in Munich, Germany, were taken hostage by terrorists from the Black September organization, a branch of the Fatah organization. Following a failed rescue attempt by the Germans, the terrorists killed all eleven Israelis.

another two or three months (around Hanukkah). Thus, if you don't change your decision that we shouldn't have personal meetings, we will only be able to see each other in several more months...

Now it's almost morning, and I still can't go to sleep. I decided to continue the letter I started several hours ago. Just when I started writing you, I heard shouts coming from the room where all the kids were sitting. I quickly went in, and they found out that the worst had happened – all eleven sportsmen, who were hostages, were killed in cold blood by the terrorists. My God! I wanted so much for this not to happen! I even prayed to God that it shouldn't happen. I was certain that everyone's prayers, mine and yours and of all your friends, would be heard and accepted, and that we would see our sportsmen coming home healthy and in one piece as if the whole thing was nothing but a bad dream. But along comes reality and blows up in our face: all the sportsmen were murdered.

The boys were quiet, very withdrawn, and several of the girls cried. I don't remember a night as sad as this. The silence was broken by Yaki, one of the boys in our group, who asked if it would not have been worth it to free terrorists imprisoned in Israel in order to prevent this terrible tragedy. After all, the terrorists wanted to exchange the sportsmen for terrorists sitting in Israeli prisons. Everybody attacked him and told him that this is not an appropriate time for debates. Yaki was insulted and went to his room, but his question continues to torment me. Maybe the entire episode could have ended differently had we freed several hundred Arab prisoners. Maybe this entire government policy, which insists on not freeing imprisoned terrorists, represents a kind of pointless stubbornness for which we have paid a terrible price, the lives of eleven wonderful boys. This question made it impossible for me to sleep, so instead of tossing and turning, I decided to get up and share my difficult thoughts and uncertainties with you. For me, you are not just Dov. You represent Judaism and Jewish history. I learned from you that our history goes back four thousand years, and even if I don't really believe that the Torah is from God, we're still talking about the accumulated wisdom of thousands of years. It's a good idea for me to hear what the Torah tells us on this topic. They must certainly have dealt with this and debated it for generations. I only hope I don't have to write you more letters under such circumstances...

Looking forward to your letter,

Talia

ב"ה

7 Tishrei 5733 [September 15, 1972]

Dear Talia,

I too was sad on Rosh Hashana. The murder of the Israeli sportsmen in Germany took me back to the days of the Holocaust. Once more, Jews are being murdered on German soil because they are Jews. Once more the world is apathetic and alienated to the murder of Jews – twenty-four hours after the murder, the games continued as usual, as though nothing had happened. It was just eleven Jews murdered. So what?

But alongside the sadness I was also happy – the world remains the same, but how different the state of the Jewish people thirty years after the Holocaust! This time, when Jews are being killed, the Jewish people have a state, they have an army, and they are capable of taking retribution on their enemies. Already on the day before Rosh Hashana, air force jets bombed terrorist bases in Lebanon, and after Rosh Hashana, I heard that dozens of terrorists were killed. The IDF's[1] operations continued in the days that followed as well – hundreds of homes of terrorists were destroyed in the course of these operations, and we also captured a large number of terrorists. What an enormous difference there is between the Jewish people in the Holocaust – "like a sheep being led to slaughter" [Isaiah

---

[1] The Israel Defense Forces, the military forces of the State of Israel.

53:7] – and the Jewish people of our own generation – "poised like a lion, to tear off arm and scalp" [Deuteronomy 33:20]. And when all is said and done, we are just one generation after the terrible Holocaust.

Talia, you know that both my mother and my father are Holocaust survivors. It is hard for them to talk about the horrors and the terrible suffering they experienced there, but sometimes something bursts forth. Throughout all the stories, a central motif is repeated: a terrible feeling of humiliation, of degradation, of their image of God being taken from them. And here God has done us this great kindness, establishing a state for us immediately after the Holocaust and giving us superhuman powers to beat all our enemies. Thanks to the statehood that God gave us, Jewish blood is no longer cheap. I recently read the marvelous essay by Rabbi Soloveitchik (a prominent Zionist rabbi in America),[2] "My Beloved Knocks." This is a really amazing essay. Among other things, Rabbi Soloveitchik describes the differences between the situation of the Jewish people before the founding of the State of Israel, and its situation following the state's establishment. Engraved in my memory is the sentence that he stresses more than any other: "Jewish blood is no longer cheap."

It is hard for me to describe how strong this feeling is, especially when I sit inside a tank (I think I told you I'm in the armored corps). Before my eyes, I see all the millions of my brothers and sisters, who were forced to run naked to the slaughter pits and the gas chambers, and I am filled with a sense of thanks to God that I am privileged to live in a generation in which God's Name is sanctified, in which the Jewish people have returned to their homeland and are defending their lives and their dignity. When we race along in tanks, storming a

---

[2] Rabbi Joseph Ber Soloveitchik (1903–1993), a scion of the Lithuanian Soloveitchik rabbinic dynasty, was a rabbi, Talmudist, and modern Jewish philosopher who headed the Rabbi Isaac Elchanan Theological Seminary of Yeshiva University in New York City and was considered a seminal figure by Modern Orthodox Jewry.

target and firing, and there is the loud noise of engines and of shells bursting, with every shell that I load into the turret I shout, "Jewish blood is not cheap!"

I am proud of our country, which, despite its being small and surrounded by enemies, knows how to defend itself heroically and not to capitulate to the extortion of wretched terrorists. I understand the emotional reaction of Yaki, who raised the possibility of preventing the murder of the sportsmen by freeing terrorists. Yet that contradicts all logic, for it is clear that surrendering once to extortion will lead to more extortion and terror, not their cessation. A normal country has to operate with intellect and not just with emotion. On this topic, I am completely in agreement with the government's policy, which totally rejected the terrorists' detestable demands.

Jewish tradition, as well, expresses fundamental opposition to surrendering to extortion, despite the great value of redeeming captives. The halachic principle is that "we do not redeem captives for more than their worth." The accepted interpretation of this is that we redeem captives only according to their commercial worth in the slave market. In other words, we pay a normal price for them and not an exaggerated price.

Yet the only issue is how much we pay, and not whether we can concede on principles and values. Forgoing values is a type of surrender that Jewish Law vociferously opposes. If a terrorist is serving a life sentence after a long legal process, and we free him after a year or two, we make a mockery of our whole legal system. Such a terrible thing certainly goes against Jewish law. The fact is that Israel's chief rabbi, Rabbi Shlomo Goren, encouraged the government in its opposition to any transaction involving freeing terrorist murderers.

I believe the best expression of the spirit of Jewish law comes not from any principle, but precisely from a man, a great Torah luminary. I am talking about Rabbi Meir of Rothenburg, or Maharam, as he is known, the spiritual leader of German Jewry about eight hundred years ago. The authorities seized him, placed him in jail, and demanded an enormous sum of money from the Jewish community in exchange for his freedom.

German Jewry responded to the call to redeem him, and within a short time all the ransom money was raised, even though it amounted to an astronomical sum in those days. When Rabbi Meir became aware of what was happening, he issued a ruling forbidding German Jewry to pay even one cent for him. The shocked Jews tried to convince him to agree to be freed, since all the money had already been collected. Yet he insisted, and taught his contemporaries and future generations: You do not surrender to extortion. After seven terrible years of torture, he died in prison, after rejecting all the entreaties of German Jewry to free him. The result was that, indeed, the phenomenon of the kidnapping of rabbis disappeared entirely from Jewish history from then until today, and a case like Maharam's has never been repeated. Imagine what would have happened had Maharam indeed given in. Any country with an empty coffer would have grabbed some rabbi and extorted from the Jews enormous sums, which would grow larger and larger. What fortitude and greatness of spirit are broadcast until this day by the story of Maharam of Rothenburg.

The State of Israel, as well, can provide a model for other countries that surrender to terror and grovel before gangs of wretched murderers.

You see that I began with sadness over the death of the eleven sportsmen, but I conclude in pride, joy, and thanks to God for the privilege we have merited of living in a generation which is "the last of subjugation and the first of redemption."

All the best,

Take care,

Dov

OCTOBER 2, 1972

Dear Dov

For me, as well, the Sukkot holiday passed with mixed feelings of sadness and pride. I share your feeling that we are allowed to be happy and proud of our country, which went out to avenge the blood of the sportsmen and killed hundreds of terrorists. But in these operations, soldiers were killed again – three soldiers were killed in Lebanon, and several days before that, two soldiers were killed on Mount Dov[1] (is this mountain named after you – just a bad joke). Is that how we are destined to live, each month losing civilians and soldiers in terror attacks and military responses?

After all, the situation has been going on almost since the beginning of Zionism, and even the state's establishment didn't change it. We thought our amazing victory in the Six-Day War would put an end to wars, and that the Arabs would resign themselves to our existence, but it turns out that we made a mistake. An ongoing war of attrition is being waged against us, and it takes a different form each time. One time it involves the shelling of the Beit She'an Valley, and another time it involves terrorists infiltrating the Jordan Valley. One time it involves battles along the Suez Canal, and another time it involves terror attacks against Israeli sportsmen. Is it decreed that we must live like this forever? Maybe it pays to give in a little? Maybe it pays to ask the Americans for help and to accept the American plans that we are rejecting all the time? Maybe we are just plain arrogant and we think we are always right? Maybe the time has come to listen to the advice that friendly countries give us? I, myself, am confused and perplexed, but I raise these doubts because they constantly bother me.

In the meantime, the one slowly emerging from her doubts is Maya. She decided that on Sukkot as well she would go to the

[1] Also known as Shebaa Farms, Mount Dov is an eight-square-mile area located southwest of the Lebanese village of Shebaa in the Golan Heights. The Shebaa Farms territory, held by Israel since 1967, is also claimed by Lebanon and Syria and is the subject of perennial dispute.

Gesher seminar at Kfar Etzion. The kibbutz did not authorize payment for the seminar, so she used all her personal savings. The counselor of her group was Hanan Porat of Kfar Etzion, and she returned full of enthusiasm. He spoke to her about a Bnei Akiva settlement group that is being formed to strengthen Kfar Etzion, and she is weighing this idea very seriously. Her parents are really worried, because they discovered that she prays every day at least once. She has joined the vegetarian table in the dining room so she won't have to eat nonkosher food. I really understand her, and I am trying to encourage her to follow the path she believes in, even if it involves a lot of hardships.

I am learning a lot of new things from your letters, and also from the people I met at Gesher, but I feel very comfortable with my life on the kibbutz. I believe it is possible to integrate the fine aspects of Jewish tradition within kibbutz life and to build something truly Zionist and Jewish. Maya no longer believes in that, and she argues against me that the situation on the kibbutz from the perspective of Jewish tradition will not improve, but will become worse. So she is preparing to cut herself off from the kibbutz and to move to a religious kibbutz. Who knows? Maybe she's really right?

With that open question, I will close.

See you,

Talia

ב"ה

5 Heshvan 5733 [October 13, 1972]

Dear Talia,

Yes, apparently, this is what is decreed for us until the messianic era. Think about the thousands of years of Jewish history and try to find a period when Jewish life was quiet and tranquil. It's kind of hard. Already the book of Genesis, which describes the life of the patriarchs and matriarchs of the Jewish people, is full of wars and struggles and unending crises. The birth of the

Jewish people occurred out of the midst of 210 years of enslavement in Egypt, followed by forty years of tortuous marching through the Sinai Desert.

But not just the nation's birth is fraught with suffering. The entire Bible is full of the wars and struggles of the Jewish people over their survival. Whoever reads Josephus's *Antiquities of the Jews* (Josephus was the Jewish historian captured by the Romans in the Great Revolt,[1] following which the Second Temple was destroyed), will see that even Jewish history during the Second Temple period was full of wars and rebellions.

And even whoever reads the monumental [Hebrew] work of Ben-Zion Dinur (an important historian, who was also the first education minister of the State of Israel), *Yisrael BaGola* [Israel in exile], will see that all the two thousand years of our exile were essentially an unending struggle to survive.

All of these struggles, obviously, involved heavy losses and bore a very heavy personal and national cost. Many grew weary and scorned this heavy price, and abandoned the Jewish people through assimilation and conversion. In the essay I mentioned in my previous letter, "My Beloved Knocks," Rabbi Soloveitchik uses the concept of "Jewish fate" to describe the history of our people. Indeed, a harsh fate has pursued us throughout our history. It is hard to be a Jew.

But the few who held on and persevered in the struggle merited to see the victory. Where are all the nations that fought against Israel, the Canaanites and the Philistines, the Ammonites and the Moabites, the Aramaeans and the Edomites? Where are all the great empires that again and again destroyed the homeland of the Jewish people – the Egyptians and the Assyrians, the Babylonians and the Persians, the Greeks and the Romans, the Byzantines and Mamluks? All of them have disappeared, descending from the stage of human history and

---

[1] The Great Revolt (66–70 CE) was a failed rebellion led by a group of Jews called the Kana'im (zealots) against the Roman occupiers of Israel, in which an estimated one million Jews died.

remaining only in museums and schoolbooks. Yet the Jewish people live on and endure, persevere in their faith and preserve their heritage, and, most importantly, they have merited to return to their ancient homeland and to reestablish their statehood anew. And the dispersed members of our people are continuing to return here from all four corners of the earth. Is that not a victory, a victory of Jewish faith over all the beliefs and religions? Was it not worth it to suffer four thousand years in order to proclaim: The Lord is God?

The big question is this: What gave those few the strength to hold out for thousands of years? Rabbi Soloveitchik's answer in that essay is one word: destiny. A great destiny and a supreme vision provide strength, sometimes almost superhuman strength, to withstand a difficult fate. Faith in God, Who gave us the Torah, and the mission of spreading that faith to all mankind, gave the Jewish people the superhuman resources to hold out against the strongest and greatest powers on earth. I am convinced that without faith, and without Torah, and without a vision of the end of days, the Jewish people would not have been able to hold out throughout the bitter exile.

That is the gist of Rabbi Soloveitchik's criticism of secular Zionism and education in the State of Israel. He argues that secular Zionism gave up on the destiny, vision, and faith that accompanied and gave strength to the Jewish people through the generations. Instead, secular Zionism made do with the goal of a "safe haven" for the Jews. (But nowhere will be safe for the Jews, Rabbi Soloveitchik maintains.) Jewish fate, which will continue to accompany us, will become unbearable, and very many Jews will seek to escape it by abandoning Judaism and Zionism together.

I do not know if you recall the harsh days of economic recession that preceded the Six-Day War. I was then already fourteen, fifteen, and remember very well the morose atmosphere, the great exit of Jews from the land, and the jokes like "Last man out, turn off the lights." Today, as well, I sense an atmosphere of bitterness and frustration rather than of joy and greatness. You gave that frustration excellent expression in your letter, when you wrote about your great disappointment that the Six-Day War did not lead to peace and calm but to a war of attrition and ongoing terror. If, God forbid, another war happens, I very much fear we will once more face an enormous wave of emigration, which is liable to be larger than that which preceded the Six-Day War.

Yes, I am very worried, and your letter worries me as well. It testifies, in my opinion, to a weariness and weakness, which endanger our continued ability to fight.

I do not reject the possibility of looking for new ways to limit the suffering and to lessen the price. There is no mitzva to die for no reason. But it is forbidden for these attempts to come at the expense of our destiny and vision. It is forbidden for us to concede our homeland, given to us by the Master of the Universe. It is forbidden for us to concede on the Jewish character of the State of Israel. It is forbidden for us to undermine the moral and legal foundations of our state by freeing terrorist murderers. These are fundamental values for the sake of which it is worth fighting, and if necessary, even dying. Life without an ideal worth dying for is not worth living.

I see no chance that the State of Israel will continue to succeed and emerge victorious unless we return to the fundamental values of the Jewish people: faith in the Creator of the Universe, a readiness to accept the Torah that He gave us, and full faith in the vision of the messianic era and the end of days. I was very happy to read in your letter that Maya is coming closer to this path, and I pray that I should see you too moving in this direction.

Be well!

Take care,

Dov

OCTOBER 24, 1972

Dear Dov,

What, have you lost your mind? You write as though you are cut off from reality. Who established the state, if not secular Jews like David Ben-Gurion? Who established the Zionist movement, if not secular Jews like Herzl?[1] What? Did Rabbi Kook establish it, or perhaps Rabbi Soloveitchik, who you talked about in your last letter? Surely, if we had all remained religious like my grandmother and grandfather, who died in the Holocaust, then the fate of us all would have been the same as theirs. It's lucky for us that there were a lot of secular Jews like the Bilu pioneers,[2] or like the members of the immigrant camps, Hapoel Hatza'ir,[3] and all sorts of other movements like those, which we learned about in history class. All of them came to Israel, built settlements, fought the British and the Arabs, and established a marvelous state. So why do you think secular Zionism has no chance of carrying on the enterprise it established? Why do you think we have become weak and weary? Is there something wrong with my thinking about how to reach a state in which the Arabs accept us and live with us in peace?

The kids in my class are now starting to talk about what happens after twelfth grade. Some want to go straight into the army, and all of them want to join elite units and become officers. Some have already received invitations to the pilots' course, and all of them are dying to succeed in that track. Is that not Zionism?

---

[1] Theodor Herzl (1860–1904), widely considered the father of modern political Zionism.

[2] Name given to members of a late nineteenth-century movement called Bilu, or the Palestine Pioneers, whose goal was the agricultural settlement of the land of Israel.

[3] Hapoel Hatza'ir (the young worker) was a Zionist youth movement founded in 1905 by the second wave of immigrants to Palestine and was active until 1930. It sought to establish a foothold in Palestine through the conquest of labor and land.

I and several other kids from our class want to take a year off before the army for a year of National Service in a development town (there is such a group in Beit She'an, and I would like to join it). Is that not Zionism? There are several kids who would like to go to the Nahal infantry brigade to strengthen our agricultural settlements in the Sinai, the Golan Heights, and the Jordan Valley. Is that not Zionism?

And in general, why do you connect everything to religion – morality is connected to religion and Zionism is connected to religion and the family is connected to religion? I don't understand why you can't be a good Jew and a good Zionist and a good Israeli even without religion. You know that I've learned over the last year to respect the religious and to understand how much power and strength there is to a life of faith, but I don't think everything depends on faith in God and mitzva observance.

The truth is that even Maya has recently started talking like you, and all day long she explains to me how without faith in God, life isn't worth living. But that really aggravates me, and I'm sorry to say that recently our relationship is cooling a bit. What a pity. Although I don't agree with you, your letters are very beautiful, and sometimes they make me think that maybe, all the same, there is something to your approach. So I ask that you keep writing as openly and sincerely and frankly as you have until now. It is really fun to read your letters, and I read them again and again.

Looking forward to your letter,

Talia

P.S. My teacher suggests that you and Hagi come for your talk with the class on Thursday, November 23. If that date suits you, tell me by phone.

ב"ה

ROSH HODESH[1] KISLEV 5733 [NOVEMBER 7, 1972]

Dear Talia,

No, I haven't lost my mind, and I don't think I am cut off from reality. Quite the contrary, I think that I am more connected to it than you are. Yes, I really think that somebody attached to the Torah is more connected to life, because I believe that our Torah is a living Torah.

Just like you, I know that Herzl established the Zionist movement and that David Ben-Gurion established the state, and I know that neither of them was religious. But you know that even the secular Ben-Gurion is very disappointed and worried by the spiritual state of Israeli society.

I recently found a very interesting book in the home of a friend of mine from my high school, Netiv Meir. He went to the army after yeshiva and completed officer training (after winning the "best soldier" award). At the end of the course, he received a gift, the book *Yihud V'Yi'ud* [Uniqueness and destiny] by David Ben-Gurion. I borrowed the book from him, and I couldn't put it down. The book includes speeches by Ben-Gurion from the period of the state's establishment. In all the speeches, the motif of the uniqueness and destiny of the Jewish people recurs. Our uniqueness, argues Ben-Gurion, is focused upon the Bible, the book of books, as he calls it, and upon the Jewish culture that developed around the Bible. The Bible presents the Jewish people with its destiny – to bequeath to the entire world the ethics of the prophets, encapsulated in the command "Love your neighbor as yourself" [Leviticus 19:18]. The destiny of the State of Israel is to fulfill this vision in practical terms. Without this vision, there is no meaning to the state's existence. Ben-Gurion emphasizes that unless we are rooted in the Bible and connected to it, we will not be able even

---

[1] Rosh Hodesh is the Hebrew term for the first day of the Hebrew month, marked by the appearance of the new moon. Rosh Hodesh has the status of a minor holiday.

to begin to fulfill this great vision. And to be connected to it means learning and teaching the Bible, studying and pondering it on all levels and in all contexts, just like the verse, "Ponder it day and night" [Joshua 1:8].

Do you think Israeli society is rooted in the Bible and ponders it day and night? Does the kibbutz you live in deal, even a little bit, with this challenge of being "rooted in the Bible and in the Jewish culture which developed around it"?

You know that on Sukkot, Hagi invited me to participate in a very interesting seminar. It was in memory of Lieutenant Yishai Ron, who fell in the Suez Canal during the War of Attrition.[2] Lecturers and Bible teachers were invited, and they addressed ways to succeed in teaching the Bible to Israeli youth. The guest of honor was David Ben-Gurion, who really attacked the Israeli educational system, which forsakes Bible study as a major topic. He recounted that when he was prime minister, he did not give up on the principle of an hour of Bible every day for every Jewish child, even though those days were days of austerity and economic troubles in Israel. He told an interesting anecdote that made everyone there burst out in laughter – Ben-Gurion removed from a cabinet meeting the minister Dov Yosef, who suggested lowering the weekly number of Bible classes from six to five, to save a bit of money. He lamented the fact that today, the number of lessons has gone down to four per week, and there are schools that have even gone down to three. He praised the religious schools, saying that specifically there Bible study is becoming stronger, and noted that in recent years, more and more students from the religious educational system are participating in the Bible contest for youth.[3]

---

[2] The War of Attrition was a limited war between Egypt and Israel that took place along the Suez Canal from 1967 until 1970, with the implementation of a cease-fire. At the end of the war, the frontiers remained largely the same as they were at the start of hostilities.

[3] This refers to the International Bible Contest, an annual competition on *Tanach* (the Old Testament) sponsored by the Israeli government and held in Jerusalem on Israel's Independence Day.

"There is no future to the State of Israel without the Bible," he burst out, shouting loudly, which really made all the participants freeze. He repeated that sentence again and again in the course of his lecture, yelling it, or almost yelling it, each time. At the end of his lecture, there were several people with questions, and the last questioner was Hagi. When he introduced himself – Hagi Ben-Artzi of Tivon – Ben-Gurion interrupted him and said to him, "You were the Bible contest winner in 1965." Hagi was shocked, and momentarily speechless. In the end, he regained his composure and asked Ben-Gurion if he didn't think that Bible study had grown weaker because it was being studied without faith in God. Could it be that it was only possible to pass on the Bible on a religious basis, and not as a merely national, moral book?

Ben-Gurion replied that he defined himself as a person who believed in God, and he thought that the Bible should be taught out of loyalty to its spirit – in other words, as a book in which the national and moral values stem from faith in God and from prophetic revelation. Yet he added that it was possible and necessary to accept the humanistic and moral values of the Bible even without faith in God, and therefore he required all the schools in Israel, religious and secular alike, to teach the Bible.

For me, this was a really exciting event, and it provided clear proof for me of just how much the Zionism of Ben-Gurion, and the entire founding generation of the state, is grounded in the Bible and connected to Jewish sources. Yet even Ben-Gurion admits that his generation did not succeed in infusing the love of the Bible and the study of the Bible in future generations, and he literally expressed trepidation over the process whereby American culture is taking over, and Jewish identity and our awareness of our "uniqueness and destiny" are being lost.

You mention your friends who wish to serve in combat units and to strengthen the Nahal encampments in the Sinai and the Golan.[4] But remember that you grew up on a lot of Bible in school and a lot of studies about our homeland, Jewish history, Hebrew literature, which is all very Zionistic. Will that atmosphere continue for another twenty or thirty years, when your children will have to decide what to do after twelfth grade?

I, like Ben-Gurion, am very wary that, together with cutting ourselves off from the Bible, we will cut ourselves off from the land of Israel as well. It may well be that your children not only will not be interested in Sinai and the Golan, but won't

First class of the Leuchter Talmud Torah in Bayit Vegan. Wearing the hat (back), *Rabbi Reuven Leuchter. Outlined* (front), *Dov; behind him, Haim Sabato.*

even be interested in the land of Israel. After all, life in America is easier and more tempting, and even safer, so why be "suckers" and remain stuck in Israel?

By the way, I think like Hagi, that without teaching the Bible as a book of faith, and without educating toward faith,

---

[4] Nahal is the name of a program in the IDF that combines military service with establishing new agricultural settlements, especially in outlying areas. Later the program branched out to include volunteering and social welfare projects.

we will not be able to pass on the Bible to future generations. I am happy about the great privilege that I and my friends have of growing up in a religious society and educating our children with the nationalistic and moral values of the Bible, out of a world of faith. I believe that only this path has a future, and every other way will lead to a dead end, with no way out.

I know that it is hard for you to accept my assessment, but you live in a very idealistic, Zionistic society. But I feel within, deeply and strongly, that this idealism and this Zionism will not hold out, and already in the next generation, or in two generations at the most, all this will crumble to dust and leave you with a broken vessel.

Hagi and I are organizing ourselves for our visit to you. This time Hagi will talk about himself and about his pathway to religion, and I will talk a bit about Jewish law and about the rationale for the mitzvot. How happy I was to hear that Maya was so inspired by Hanan Porat and is weighing the possibility of going with a Bnei Akiva settlement group to Kfar Etzion. Why shouldn't you join her and have a taste of life within religious society? Maybe you'll like it? The book of Psalms says: "Taste and see that God is good" [Psalms 34:9], and a word to the wise is sufficient.

Hoping to see you soon,

Dov

NOVEMBER 16, 1972

Dear Dov,

The meeting with you (for which Maya and I are already waiting impatiently) was almost, almost canceled. Our teacher suggested we postpone it by several weeks, because before Hanukkah we're starting exams, and this year we are taking our matriculation exams, and our studies are going into high gear, etc., etc., etc. We felt like she was just looking for excuses to cancel the

meeting with you. We decided not to give in. We took the bus –
Maya and me – to her home (she lives in the next kibbutz), and
poured out our hearts to her. We told her we felt she was looking for excuses to cancel your visit to the kibbutz, and that we
were not willing to take that lying down.

For the first time we told her what we think about the way
the kibbutz shuts itself off from the outside. We are no better
than most extremist haredim [strictly Torah-observant Jews].
In our kibbutz as well, there is not one religious teacher in the
whole school. No one has tried to show us that there are other
pathways in life, that there are other worlds, and that it is possible to learn the Bible without biblical criticism, but rather in
the traditional way, with Rashi and the Midrashim of our sages.
People always make fun of the religious and scorn the Haredim,
and everything connected to religion is automatically presented as primitive and old-fashioned.

We told her that during the past year we have discovered,
through the Gesher seminars, and through my corresponding
with you, religious people who are no less enlightened than us,
and no less Zionistic than us, and also no less friendly than us.
We've discovered an interesting, serious world that confronts
the most modern challenges in life. And, when all is said and
done, this is our culture, the culture of the Jewish people for
thousands of years, so why are they trying so hard to cut us off
from it?

The truth is that she was quite shocked by our attack, and her
answers were quite confused and quite outrageous. She hinted
to us that Maya's parents are really hysterical and are exercis-
ing heavy pressure on the school not to authorize your visit
(Maya told me that she will get back at her parents over this).
Her parents know that her move to the vegetarian table in the
kibbutz dining room has to do with the *kashrut* laws and is not
a matter of ethics or dieting. Apparently there are other parents who share their apprehension that such visits will agitate
things too much and cause their children to have thoughts of
becoming religious. In short, we succeeded in nullifying the evil

decree, and our teacher has agreed for you to come as planned next week. She asked that we convey to you the following instructions:

1. Not to talk at all about Hagi's becoming religious

2. Not to criticize the kibbutz or the school

3. You should discuss topics like: religious coercion, religious legislation, people prohibited by Jewish law from marrying (e.g., a *kohen*[1] with a divorcée, etc.) and problems resulting with their children being classed as *mamzerim*,[2] the military service of yeshiva students and religious girls, etc.

We understand that our teacher wants to push you into a corner where it will be easy for her to attack you and it will be hard for you to defend yourselves. If that doesn't suit you, you can cancel the meeting. Maya and I will be very sorry, but we'll understand. Now the ball is in your court.

Looking forward to seeing you,

Talia

NOVEMBER 25, 1972

Dear Dov,

How happy I am that the meeting on Thursday went okay. I was very afraid that our teacher was preparing a trap for you. I was especially afraid because last week all the newspapers and all the radio programs were only talking about *mamzerim*,[3] and I

---

[1] Literally, "priest," the term *kohen* refers to a Jew who is a direct patrilineal descendant of the biblical Aaron and is bound by additional obligations and restrictions within Jewish law. *Kohanim* performed the service of sacrificial offerings in the times of the Temple.

[2] A *mamzer* is a person born of an adulterous or incestuous union. Marriages between *mamzerim* and non-*mamzerim* are largely forbidden by Jewish law.

[3] On November 20, 1972, Rabbi Shlomo Goren, then the Ashkenazic chief rabbi, married Chanoch and Miriam Langer to their respective partners after nullifying a previous decision of the rabbinic courts that classified them as *mamzerim*.

was sure the whole discussion would focus on that. I was happy that you were not alarmed when they brought up the issue of *mamzerim*, and instead of getting into a debate, you gave information that even the teacher did not have. We suddenly realized that we lack so much basic knowledge about Judaism, and that our opposition to religion and to religious Jews often derives from lack of knowledge and even from boorishness.

On the topic of *mamzerim* you were lucky, because Rabbi Goren courageously solved the problem of that brother and sister (in the news), and a lot of secular Jews praised him for that. But regarding the subject of a *kohen* marrying a divorcée, you spoke about the holiness of *kohanim* and about the Temple, and I was not able to understand why marrying a divorcée is something unholy that works against the job of the *kohanim* in the Temple. I, as a woman (albeit unmarried), am very insulted by this attitude toward a divorcée. On our kibbutz we have several divorced women who did not get along with their husbands, but they are excellent women who could create wonderful families with another man. Why don't you, the religious, have the courage to admit that Judaism contains old-fashioned elements inappropriate to our times, even if, perhaps, they were appropriate in other times and under other conditions. I don't think that even in the times of the Temple it was necessary to relate this way to a divorcée, but in our times there certainly is no place for such an insulting approach.

On our kibbutz, we have one couple that got married in Cyprus, because he is a *kohen* in a second marriage, to a woman who is herself a divorcée. They are actually a very nice couple, and they have two very sweet children. So why be against such a thing?

Maya as well told me that in her opinion, you did not have a convincing explanation on this topic, and she too wants to hear your view on the possibility of changing the halakha.

All in all, it's good that you came, because a lot of kids left the talk with a bit more humility, since they saw that they lack a lot of knowledge. I hope that in the future, before they attack the religious or religion, they'll first try to get the facts and accept verified information from someone who really understands Judaism.

It is also good that the bus came late because of the rain, so that we had several minutes to talk with each other, and I hope, Dov, that you don't have too many guilt feelings over that. Thanks again for coming.

Take care,

Talia

ב"ה

3 Tevet 5733 [December 7, 1972], Eighth Night of Hanukkah

Dear Talia,

I am writing to you as I sit before the Hanukkah candles, which remind us of the great struggle between Jewish faith and Greek culture during the Second Temple period. Greek philosophy believed in the absolute power of the human intellect, and Judaism, by contrast, recognized the limitations of the human intellect. Due to those limitations, we need the Torah, which came to us through divine revelation. Thus, not everything in the Torah can be understood by way of the human intellect, and certainly not fully and absolutely. All the same, I make an effort to understand the mitzvot of the Torah as much as I can, for the Torah says, "It is the proof of our wisdom and understanding in the eyes of the nations" [Deuteronomy 4:6]. In his *Guide for the Perplexed*, Rambam (you must certainly know by now who he is) understands this verse as teaching about our duty to make an effort to understand and also to try to explain every mitzva of the Torah through human wisdom.

The *kohanim* during the time of the Temple did not just serve in the Temple. They also taught the Torah to the public at large. The Bible states, "For the lips of a priest guard knowledge, and men seek rulings from his mouth" [Malachi 2:7]. The kohanim are the teachers of Torah, the rabbis of the biblical period. Their main function of teaching the people Torah was carried out in Jerusalem, when the entire nation came to the Temple during the three pilgrimage festivals: Pesach, Shavuot, and Sukkot. During those holidays, they not only brought offerings and held festive celebrations; the mass gathering presented an opportunity to teach the Torah to the gathered pilgrims.

Jewish tradition views the teacher not only as a conduit for the transfer of knowledge, but as a source of inspiration, holiness, and faith. He has to be a paragon of virtue in his personal life so that he will also be worthy to teach Torah. A teacher is also an educator, and education occurs first and foremost through the personal example of the teacher. One of the main components of the personal example lies in the realm of the teacher's family life. He has to exemplify someone who has established a strong, stable family, unblemished, God forbid, by divorce or other terrible occurrences.

Why is a divorcée unsuitable for a *kohen*? Because somebody who has already gotten divorced one time may *possibly* have a problematic personality, so that she is hard to get along with, and that is why he or she got divorced. I emphasize the word "possibly." The divorce is certainly not absolute proof of a problem, and the probability of a problem may be low, but the possibility exists. The Torah apparently wants to lessen the likelihood of divorce in the families of *kohanim*, who are, as noted, the families that need to provide a personal example to the community.

Obviously, it may well be that most divorced women are excellent people who got divorced due to incompatibility with their spouse, or due to the spouse's personal problems. Yet there is also a possibility, which cannot be discounted, that the divorce occurred because of the woman, that her character or behavior led to the family breaking up. So if we want *kohanim* to go and establish their families in a secure manner, why take unnecessary risks?

It's like driving a new car as opposed to a secondhand car that has already been in an accident. True, even the car that has been in the accident can be fixed up so that it will work beautifully, but a person who doesn't want to take a risk will forgo it.

The Torah does not demand these high standards of every Jew, but only of *kohanim*, who are the nation's teachers and educators. Jews who are not *kohanim*, comprising the vast majority of Jews, can wed a divorcée without any limitations. Thus, we are talking about a limitation that is not very significant in terms of the chance that a divorcée will wed *once more*. (Let me say parenthetically that, in my opinion, even a Jew who is not a *kohen* should investigate well before he marries a divorcée, in order to negate the possibility that she has a problematic personality that will lead to the dissolution of the marital bond.)

You can go on and ask a question, that this may have been all well and good in the time of the Temple, but what does it have to do with our own times, in which there are teachers and rabbis who are not *kohanim*, and most *kohanim* do not work specifically in education? You are right, if the Temple belongs to the past. But if somebody believes that the Temple belongs to the future as well, and prays every day that "the Temple should be rebuilt soon in our day," then he cannot so quickly forgo the laws involving the Temple. The *kohanim* and *levi'im*[1] no doubt constitute a central component of the Temple experience. It is therefore so important for the Jewish people to preserve the lineage of the *kohanim*, as well as the laws and customs associated with them.

All in all, I am sometimes jealous of the *kohanim*, who, with God's help, will soon be privileged to be once again the group that educates the Jewish people. I too would like to be included in this group, and, in this regard, I feel that I am very privileged to be part of that marvelous group of yeshiva

---

[1] Descendants of the tribe of Levi, from which *kohanim* are also descended. *Levi'im*, like *kohanim*, have specific rights and obligations according to Jewish law and were charged with special duties in the Temple.

students who are preparing themselves for positions as teachers and educators of the Jewish people.

I thank you, Talia, for the privilege you gave me of coming to your kibbutz and talking to your class. I pray that, with God's help, I will be privileged in the future to have contact with a large secular public in order to bring them closer to faith and to Torah. I feel that God has blessed me with resources suited to this great and holy mission, and I am investing all of my energies and efforts during these years to prepare myself to fulfill this important mission. Hagi, as well, is preparing himself to educate the secular public, and perhaps we will be privileged to work together.

Warm regards to Maya and to all of your classmates. It was an excellent meeting.

Take care,

Dov

DECEMBER 19, 1972

Dear Dov,

Your explanation about the prohibition on marriage between a *kohen* and a divorcée is very interesting, and only now do I understand what you said at our meeting. There was sometimes so much noise that I didn't hear what you were saying, especially since you were talking quietly.

But I am still resentful regarding the religious coercion in this matter, as in other matters in the realm of family life. If a religious *kohen* believes in all of these laws, then he should not marry a divorcée or any other woman that the Torah makes forbidden to him. But why does the state have to force these laws on secular *kohanim* who do not believe in all these laws? Why should a *kohen* who wants to marry a divorcée have to go to Cypress or elsewhere abroad? Why can't he get married in our country like a normal person?

I also don't understand why you people are so stubborn about this coercion. When all is said and done, a secular *kohen* who wants to marry a divorcée will go abroad and he will do it. All you've "earned" in the end is one more person who hates religion and rabbis. So what do you need that for? Let everyone marry and divorce however they please, and I am certain that it will very much reduce the great tension that exists between the religious and the secular in the State of Israel.

I am happy that you are proud to be part of the body of yeshiva students, but I don't understand why these boys deserve an exemption from army service. Why don't they have to contribute like all other boys in this country, who sometimes sacrifice their lives for its sake? There are many thousands of students who are preparing themselves for very important roles in this country, like engineers and physicians and scientists and economists. Even so, not one of them says that he has to be exempt from army service. Why do only the yeshiva students have to be exempt from this duty? (I learned from you to say "this holy duty.")

You told us that you learn in a yeshiva in which the students both study Torah and serve in the army, but, if I understood you right, even you don't do full three-year service like every young Israeli, but only about a year and a half (correct me if I am wrong). Why do you deserve to enjoy a shorter service? Are your studies more important than those of a physician, who saves lives, or of an engineer, who builds the country?

I hope you are not insulted by these questions. I very much value your service in the Armored Corps and Hagi's service in the Artillery Corps, but you have to feel uncomfortable about this disparity.

Looking forward to your answer,

Take care,

Talia

ב"ה

ROSH HODESH SHVAT [JANUARY 4, 1973]

Dear Talia,

You're right. I too think yeshiva students have to serve in the army and do their share to defend the country. I can never forget what Moses said to the tribes who wished to remain on the eastern bank of the Jordan when Israel was about to enter the land and conquer it: "Are your brothers to go to war while you remain here?" [Numbers 32:6]. Let me tell you something. Taking part in a compulsory war is so important that the Mishna says even "a newlywed bride and groom set out for war from their wedding celebration" [Sota 8:7]. Even a groom, who is exempt following the wedding ceremony from reciting the Shema, is not exempt from going off to war.

That's exactly why I decided to go to a yeshiva in which Torah study is combined with military service, and not to one whose students do not enlist. You know that after yeshiva high school I thought about continuing in Yeshivat Knesset Hizkiyahu in Kfar Hasidim. The yeshiva is considered excellent in terms of the level of its studies and lectures. Hagi, as well, learned there for about a year, enjoyed it very much, and advanced scholastically. Ultimately, however, I decided to continue in Kerem B'Yavneh because of the *hesder* program, which integrates three stints of military service in its study program.

Our track is modeled along the lines of the Nahal track – basic training, advanced training, and operational deployment. The difference between us and the Nahal soldiers is that when they head off to the pioneering settlements or the kibbutz, we go back to the yeshiva to study Torah.

Obviously, the same question can be asked about the Nahal track: Why do the Nahal soldiers give only a year and a half of active service, while raising tomatoes in the Jordan Valley the rest of the time? The state's answer is that settling the Jordan Valley is a national mission so important that the state is ready to forgo part of military service in favor of settling areas important to national security. The state answers similarly regarding the *hesder* yeshivot: studying Torah and preparing a new generation of Zionistic teachers and educators who have both studied Torah and served in the army is a national mission so great and important that the state is ready to forgo part of military service for it.

In terms of military training, we receive full combat training like all the Nahal soldiers without cutting any corners. We did full infantry training at Camp 80 next to Hadera for a year and a half. That was not easy in the least, and almost everybody completed it. Until my year, most of the hesderniks would advance to paratroopers and do advanced training in Battalion 50 of the Nahal paratroopers. Starting with my year, the army decided that it is more important to strengthen the armored corps, so they sent all of us to the full armored track – a professional tank course, and after that TPC, "Team-Platoon-Company" – where we apply all we learned. Some of us also went to the tank commanders course. I, personally, did not feel I was suited to command, so I preferred to remain a simple soldier, and I hope I will be privileged to serve my country to my utmost, even as a simple soldier.

The only sphere in which our military contribution is incomplete is in becoming commanders and officers. Hagi, for example, wanted to go to artillery officer training following his advanced training course, but the head of our yeshiva did not let him do it. Hagi gave up on this, but he told me he wants to join the standing army after he completes *hesder*, and to do officer training.

All in all, you've got to remember that most military service is performed in reserve duty. In the course of twenty-five or thirty years of reserve duty, every soldier gives at least as much time in reserve duty as he gave in his three-year compulsory service, and maybe even more. In reserve duty, we serve exactly like all the other combat soldiers, and many graduates of our yeshiva participated as paratroopers in the liberation of Jerusalem during the Six-Day War.

Educationally, I see the *hesder* yeshivot as filling a crucial role. You must certainly know that the Jews of the Enlightenment accused the rabbis and yeshiva students that their Torah was cut off from life. You must certainly have studied Bialik's[1] story "The *Masmid*" [the diligent scholar], containing a description of the yeshiva student as closed off behind the walls of the yeshiva and its books.

Rabbi Kook, who moved to Eretz Yisrael about seventy years ago, tried his utmost to close this divide and create a link between the world of Torah and the national challenges of the land of Israel. And today it is happening – the *hesder* yeshivot prove that it is possible to join Torah and army service and to produce yeshiva students who know both how to learn and teach Torah and how to be good combat soldiers who contribute to the nation's security. In my opinion, it is important to extend this connection to other realms as well, such as Torah and science. This year, Hagi is studying at Bar-Ilan University, and he told me that a *beit midrash* [house of study] has been set up there, where students combine Torah study in the morning with the study of science in the afternoon. I believe we will see this connection expand to other realms as well – Torah and technology, Torah and communications, and perhaps Torah and medicine.

Rabbi Kook calls this Torah, which is connected to life, Torat Eretz Yisrael, the Torah of the land of Israel, because it develops only in the natural place of the Jewish people. Only at home can a person live a normal, natural life; hence, only in Eretz Yisrael is the Torah once more becoming what it really is, a living Torah linked to all realms of human activity. Today the *hesder* yeshivot, more than anything else, express this revolution.

---

[1] Hayim Nahman Bialik (1873–1934) was a Russian-born Jew who left his religious upbringing to follow the ideals of the Enlightenment. He went on to become one of the pioneers of modern Hebrew poetry and came to be regarded as Israel's national poet.

I am happy for the opportunity that has come my way to be a partner in this revolution, which I believe will produce Torah scholars of a kind entirely different from all those we knew in the exile. I also believe that this new image that will sprout from the world of Torah will connect itself to the new Jew that Zionism tried to create. This will allow the Zionist revolution to reattach itself to the world of Torah, from which it was cut off because of the rebellion against the exile and the exilic mentality that religious communities often adhered to. In other words: you, the kibbutzniks, who led the Zionist revolution, will be able to reattach yourselves to the Torah via the *hesder* yeshivot.

Right now, you must for sure be saying to yourself, "Look, Dov is at it again, trying to turn me religious." You know what? Correct! You're right on this point too. That's exactly why it is important to me to build and strengthen the *hesder* track, because I don't believe you will ever be able to attach yourselves to the Torah of Bnei Brak and Meah She'arim.[2] My responsibility to the Jewish people obligates me to create a new model of a yeshiva student and Torah scholar, with whom you will not only be able to find common topics for discussion, but in whom you will find all the values of Zionism and the Enlightenment.

Hagi told me that this was the "shock" that led him to become religious. He was sure that yeshiva students only learn Torah, and that they are narrow-minded, provincial, and closed. Then he visited a yeshiva high school and discovered the students there to be as enlightened and broad-minded as he is. He was certain that yeshiva students don't do army service (and this angered him just like it angers you), until he visited Yeshivat Kerem B'Yavneh and discovered yeshiva students who are also paratroopers (with a red beret and shiny paratrooper wings, the dream of every Israeli youth).

---

[2] Bnei Brak, a city located just east of Tel Aviv, and Meah She'arim, one of the oldest neighborhoods in Jerusalem, are both populated mainly by haredi Jews and are considered centers of Ultra-Orthodox Judaism.

Talia, you cannot imagine how happy I was to hear that Maya wants to join the Nahal settlement group of Bnei Akiva at Kfar Etzion. I sometimes dream of receiving a letter from you with just three words: "I'm with Maya."

With that sweet dream I am going to sleep.

Be well, and see you,

Dov

P.S. I'll write about religious coercion in another letter. Right now I've run out of strength to write any more.

ב"ה

4 SHVAT 5733 [JANUARY 7, 1973]

Dear Talia,

I've got a bad conscience over not having dealt with religious coercion in my last letter, so I decided to fill in what was missing before I receive another letter from you. You ask, justly: Why doesn't our state allow even couples that are halachically ineligible to wed (like a *kohen* with a divorcée) to undergo a civil ceremony in the State of Israel, as is accepted in all the democratic countries of the world?

You know that the real problem is not people ineligible to wed, like a *kohen* with a divorcée. Those constitute only a small number of cases, and it is really not worth fighting over them and creating such great tension between the religious and the secular. In all the cases of people ineligible to wed, where both are Jewish, the children too are valid Jews and the problem is really very limited.

The real problem involves marriages between Jews and non-Jews. It is clear that if Israel makes civil ceremonies an option, then sooner or later even religiously mixed couples, a Jew and a non-Jew, will be able to wed this way. Such mixed marriages are a tragedy for the Jewish people. Assimilation in the Diaspora is reaching alarming proportions. In Jewish communities in Europe, we are already talking about most Jews marrying a non-Jewish spouse, and even in America, mixed marriages are approaching 50 percent. This process is simply wiping out the Jewish people, because the children of these couples are either non-Jews from a *halachic* perspective (when the mother is a non-Jewess), or non-Jews culturally and educationally (in 95 percent of the cases).

I recently read an article by an expert on Jewish demography, Professor Sergio Della Pergola (that's a funny name!). He argues that American Jewry lose a million Jews every ten years through assimilation alone.

In Israel, as well, the problem of mixed marriages is starting to worsen due to the huge wave of volunteers who came here after the war (I think you told me there are mixed marriages on your kibbutz, as well).

Regarding this critical, existential issue, the State of Israel, as the national and cultural center of the Jewish people, needs to broadcast a clear message that it disapproves of and objects to this process. It cannot be that a Jewish state will allow such marriages officially, with state approval. The meaning of such a possibility is the legitimization of mixed marriages.

Even if we don't think in religious or halachic terms, the process of assimilation and mixed marriages constitutes an existential threat even from a national perspective. What will the Jews of the exile think if mixed families such as these show up with an official document with the Temple candelabra emblazoned on it, which, as is known, is the symbol of the State of Israel? It's forbidden for us to do such a thing.

The compromise that was worked out (in the language of the media, "the status quo") was that if such couples wed abroad by civil marriage, then the Jewish state will recognize them as families in every sense of the word. By such means, the human problem is solved, because the state gives such couples all the services essential to a family (housing mortgages, medical insurance, etc.), but it does not officially legitimize this process.

I think this stubborn insistence on not legitimizing assimilation has great educational meaning. In my opinion, even a nonobservant person who hopes for the welfare and preservation of the Jewish people has to want this compromise to continue. It is not just in the interest of the religious. Quite the contrary, it may be even more in the interest of the secular, for they are more exposed to the dangers of assimilation and mixed marriages.

In the eleventh grade at Yeshivat Netiv Meir. Front row, l to r: Uri Seri, Dr. Schwartz. Middle row, l to r: Digman, Rabbi Yossi Ben Shachar, Dov Indig (boxed), Haim Sabato (boxed), Professor Simha Feigelstein (bending down). Back row, l to r: Danny Teperberg (second from left), Professor Menachem Ben-Sasson (today president of the Hebrew University of Jerusalem), Higash (up higher), Shlomo Raziel (partially obscured behind Feigelstein), Gutman (partially obscured behind Raziel).

You, obviously, can suggest separating between Jews *halachically* ineligible to wed and mixed marriage. In other words, you can demand that Jews ineligible to wed be permitted to marry (like a *kohen* and a divorcée) and marriages between mixed couples (Jew and non-Jew) continue to be forbidden. Yet I do not believe that making such a distinction is practical and will endure. Once there is a civil marriage track, it will operate and develop according to its own internal logic, viewing every couple as a legitimate family even if they don't belong to the same religion, as is normal in democratic countries.

I hear you groaning and saying to yourself, "Enough! When will we be a normal, secular, democratic country already, like the progressive countries of Europe or America?" And I say to you, Talia, that if all we wanted was to establish a normal country, it wasn't worth establishing the State of Israel, and it isn't worth continuing to fight for its existence. We'd be better off packing up and moving to America or Australia. There it is safer, easier, and there are Jewish communities there, for those interested in preserving their Jewishness.

If the State of Israel is a Jewish state, in which the life, culture, and spirit of the Jewish people are being renewed, in which the Jewish people are living their ideals and heritage, in which the Jewish people are strengthening their Jewish identity and developing it, then it's worth living here, and even fighting if necessary (and even dying for it, if it is so decreed). It doesn't pay to do this for the sake of a second America in the Middle East. There is already one America and you don't need another, which, when all is said and done, will just be a poor imitation of the original.

I've written enough for a second letter within one week (I don't think I'll be writing you until you answer me. Now it's your turn to write two letters, one after the other).

Regards to Maya,

Take care,

Dov

JANUARY 19, 1973

Dear Dov,

What can I say? You're amazing! You managed to carry yourself well on two topics (drafting yeshiva students and civil marriage) when I didn't expect you to come out of it in one piece. It's a shame you didn't have a chance to present your position on these two topics before the class. I'm certain that many would have changed their minds. Me, for sure, you convinced that the religious position on civil marriage not only has religious logic, but very strong logic from a national standpoint as well.

I still don't understand why the religious insist on preventing us secular Jews from spending Shabbat the way we want. Are you going to tell me that if public transportation runs on Shabbat, then the state isn't Jewish? (True, with us in Haifa in the north, buses run on Shabbat, but in most of the country they don't.) If a family goes to visit Grandma and Grandpa on Shabbat, what's so awful about that? What's not Jewish about it? And even if they do take a trip on Shabbat, isn't that a nice way to spend it, and to strengthen the family bond?

Also the laws that close down all the stores on Shabbat make me angry. Shabbat is the only free day during the week, and it suits me to do my shopping then, or just to walk around among the stores and to see nice things. You religious people are busy all of Shabbat. You go to synagogue and hear lectures. At the Gesher seminar, every Shabbat meal lasted at least two hours, with lots of singing and Torah thoughts.

We, however, get up on Saturday morning (at ten instead of seven) and we look for something to do, and it turns out that we're grounded. Anyone without a car is stuck. And if someone does have a car, you can't take advantage of it for shopping, even emergency shopping. Who needs it? I'm sure that if you all announced you have no objection to secular Jews fashioning Shabbat in this country according to their wishes, a lot of tension and anger that we all feel toward you would instantaneously be freed up. You, obviously, can continue living your lives according to your faith without anybody bothering you. What's the problem with that? And please, don't spout your funny proclamation again about how, if that's how things are, then it wasn't worth establishing the Jewish state and it isn't worth fighting for it.

My parents are Holocaust survivors (and I think yours are too). They fled to here because in Europe all of their families and relatives were killed, and no country would take them but the State of Israel. What do you want? For us to return to Europe so they can carry out a second Holocaust on us? Even if this country doesn't have anything Jewish except for the fact that it takes in any Jew in distress from anywhere on the face of the earth – this in itself justifies the state's establishment and the struggle for its survival.

What's with you and America? You're always mentioning it, as though it's the ideal solution for secular Jews. That isn't so. Even secular Jews have Jewish feelings. Even they feel that Eretz Yisrael is our homeland, the home from which we were banished thousands of years ago, and the home to which we are now returning. Look how many secular Jews come to the Western Wall, go to the Tomb of the Patriarchs in Hebron, and even go to pray at Rachel's Tomb. And yes, even we get emotional there. So why should we want to immigrate to America? If there are buses on Shabbat and we can live a normal life here, precisely that will increase the desire of many Jews to remain in Israel and to live here. In short, please don't wave America under my nose all the time.

And besides that, America has lots of criminals and frightening street gangs. I heard from one of the girls on the kibbutz who moved here from America (Chicago), that people there are really afraid to leave their homes at night. So what's so bad about Israel for us? We can move around freely in Haifa until midnight without fear (there's no choice – you've got to come home at midnight, because that's when the last bus runs). And since now it's already almost midnight, I'm signing off.

Good night,

Take care,

Talia

ב"ה

30 Shvat 5733 [February 2, 1973]

Dear Talia,

Let's say that I accept your proposal – public transportation (buses, trains, and planes) operates on Shabbat, all the stores and the shopping centers are open, all the entertainment spots and all the media systems are working full steam. Perhaps later on, any factory owner who wants to operate his factory on Shabbat will be able to do so. Think about what the result will be.

First of all, no religious Jew will be able to work in any of these systems, not in the bus companies, not in El Al, not in Israeli television, and not in the Israeli cinema. Is that why we established a Jewish state, so that a religious Jew would be unable to work in transportation or media, which serve the public at large in this country? Is the State of Israel just a continuation of the exile, in which a religious Jew feels himself to be ostracized and excluded?

I am thinking about an even worse result. A lot of Israelis are traditional. They aren't actually religious, but they preserve our traditions. They don't work on Shabbat, they keep kosher, at least at home, they go to the synagogue on the High Holidays, etc. What will happen to such a person when he is faced with a choice: to work on Shabbat or to be fired? I assume that many traditional Jews will not give up their workplaces, and will be forced to work against their conscience.

Is that not antireligious coercion? In the same context, I'm bothered by a much worse problem: What will happen if they open the stores on Shabbat? Those stores that do not open on Shabbat will suffer a major blow. It will be a case of unfair competition. And if you say, "That's *their* problem," I'll answer you, "It's *our* problem, the problem of us all." Did we establish a Jewish state so religious Jews would once more be pushed into a corner and would once more face unjust discrimination? Once again, I fear for those traditional merchants who are liable to open their stores on Shabbat due to the fierce economic competition. Here we are in a horror movie in which even in a

Jewish state a Jew cannot rest on Shabbat, and is actually being forced to work on Shabbat. For me, this really is a horror movie, a nightmare. To my mind, the religious public has to storm the barricades to prevent such a situation from developing. You know what? The traditional public should too, because it's in fact them that are much more likely to be dragged into working on Shabbat than the religious public.

You know, Talia? The thing I am most afraid of in this context is this: If, God forbid, you succeed in secularizing Shabbat in the Jewish state, two economic networks will develop in this country – Shabbat-observant stores, and Shabbat-observant factories. The religious will not enter the stores of the irreligious, nor will they buy from their factories (after all, we will have to help our religious brethren to survive the economic war and the unjust competition). Do you understand what the unavoidable result will be? The delicate, fragile fabric that connects us as one people with an awareness of mutual and shared responsibility will unravel. If, God forbid, you succeed in establishing civil marriage as well, then we will have to separate ourselves from you both in the army and in other joint frameworks. Did I mention two peoples? Well, that's exactly what will happen.

Believe me, Talia, if, God forbid, you succeed in turning our precious country, which through God's kindness we succeeded in establishing after two thousand years of exile, into one more Western, secular country, you, the secular, will be the first to run away from it. I am well aware of the Zionist argument about anti-Semitism in the exile, an argument which unfortunately proved itself big time during the Holocaust. You don't have to convince me. I hope to stay here even if things become a lot harder, because such is my faith and such is the mitzva obligating me as a religious Jew.

It's you who have the problem of secular youth encountering a modern world that today graciously accepts the Jew almost everywhere, especially in America. America is a country of immigrants, where all the races, religions, and ethnic groups mix together. Within that atmosphere of equality and democracy, even Jews feel, perhaps for the first time in history, equal and desired participants. There, everything is always going to be bigger, more profitable, more convenient, safer. Little Israel, surrounded by hundreds of millions of Arabs who seek its destruction, will never be able to compare to America in the economic or security realm. We have only one thing we can offer, which doesn't exist anywhere else in the world, and that is a Jewish state. Here, you can feel what Shabbat is and what Yom Kippur is. Here, your children are protected from assimilation (at least relatively), and they soak up Jewish culture, even on the street and even in school.

Believe me, Talia, if these things are important to a person, he will remain here, even if, God forbid, the economic and security situation gets worse. And if these things are not important to him, sooner or later he'll fall prey to temptation and find himself making up excuses why he is in California or Florida. I know it is hard for you to understand me, but I feel these things very strongly. And I am sharing with you everything I feel openly and candidly, just like we promised each other at the start of our correspondence.

It really hurts me to write you these things, because I know you feel entirely different – you are a Jew and a Zionist with all your being. I write you these words thinking chiefly about your children in another twenty or thirty years. Will they feel themselves Jews and Zionists the way you do? This is the question that constantly bothers me. And because it bothers me so much, I'm willing to give up so many hours of sleep for its sake, and instead of sleeping, I sit and write you under a small night-light so as not to wake up my roommates. Is my investment worth it? I'm sure it is, because every letter I receive from you gives me the feeling that every word I have written to you has been read more than once. But now I've really gone too far (it's three o'clock in the morning), so good night until next time.

Take care,

Dov

103

FEBRUARY 11, 1973

Dear Dov,

This is the first time, really the first time, that you made me cry. I sat with your letter and with the questions that you raised in it: How will my children grow up? Will they want to stay in Israel? Will they feel themselves Jews at least as much as I do? Suddenly I discovered that I am incapable of answering these questions, and since I was alone in my room, I let myself cry a little.

Totally without warning, Maya came into the room. She saw me with red eyes and she hugged me very hard. I let her read your letter (because you never ever wrote me that I'm not allowed to give her your letters). She read quietly, and when she finished, she looked at me and she said one sentence: "It's because of these questions that I'm going to Kfar Etzion." After several minutes she added another sentence: "Maybe you'll come with me?" Suddenly I found myself crying even harder. How important Maya is to me, and how I have wanted that we continue to be together after high school! And then she decides that she's cutting herself off from us, that she is taking another path that she believes in. I lack the strength to take her path. I don't have her belief. I don't have her enthusiasm. Maybe I don't think as deeply as she does. She reads books all the time. She corresponds with Hanan Porat from Kfar Etzion, who was her counselor. She meets with girls from Haifa who were with us on the Gesher seminar. In short, she is strong and she is stubborn, and apparently, even her parents have given up. If only I had the same strength she does!

With red eyes and a wet letter, I await your letters to me.

Talia

P.S. I too am going to be doing something important. I've decided to volunteer before the army for a year of service in Beit She'an. There, I'm supposed to be helping children having difficulties in school. I will also be helping illiterate elderly people to master basic skills in reading and writing. Next week we'll be having a tour of Beit She'an with several other kids from the group going there. I am really excited about our first meeting with the people who I'll be working with next year. Those matriculation exams are starting to look not so important to me.

FEBRUARY 22, 1973

Dear Dov,

Yesterday I was in Beit She'an with everyone who's going there next year for the year of service. The whole group looks really cool without exception. They're all full of motivation to invest and contribute as much as they can. I was less impressed by the population we're supposed to be working with. They were quite suspicious of us. The children were sweet and full of curiosity, but the adults were a little distant and sometimes even hostile. One of the old men we met asked the boys in the group if they put on tefillin. When they answered that they didn't, he responded quite angrily: "So what could you possibly be teaching me? I need to teach you!" Another added: "What kind of Jews are you if you don't put on tefillin?" In short, it was quite an embarrassing moment. Otherwise, however, the scenery in Beit She'an is beautiful and the dates we got were sweeter than honey.

Some came back from the tour with second thoughts – maybe they would go straight to the army after all. But I'm determined to try this route, because if there is no connection between kibbutz members and the youth of Beit She'an, then we really will become two peoples in this country. We've got to insist on this connection. And as you can see, I too am stubbornly keeping up my connection with you. So write more.

Take care,

Talia

ב"ה

2 ADAR II 5733 [MARCH 6, 1973]

Dear Talia,

Hurray! I'm a soldier! We were drafted for the third haul of our military service, which will last a half a year almost until Rosh Hashana. Every time I put on my uniform and receive my rifle I'm filled with joy and pride and strength. My parents' families were murdered in the Holocaust by the cursed Germans – may their names be blotted out! They were powerless, without any possibility of fighting for their lives. We, however, thank G-d, were very privileged in a way that they were not. We returned to our homeland; established our country, the country of the Jewish people; and we built the IDF. What pride I feel with my weapon in my hand! I can fight for my life, defend my home, protect my homeland against all those who rise up against us (and they, unfortunately, are very great in number).

This tremendous change gives me a lot of faith, faith in the God of Israel. Who knows if we would have been able to carry on as believing Jews after the horrible Holocaust if the State of Israel had not arisen? Yet it did arise, and suddenly we saw with our own eyes all the enormous miracles – the astounding victories over the Arab armies in the War of Independence, the Sinai Campaign, and the Six-Day War; the great aliya and the ingathering of the exiles from all parts of the globe; the flourishing of Eretz Yisrael in all economic spheres. The divine promise has been fulfilled and has become a living reality after two thousand years of exile, and together with it, our faith has been revived and strengthened as well. And perhaps there was no way to achieve a state other than through the Holocaust, through the awful shock that it caused both the Jewish people and the nations. Do you know what? Rabbi Tzvi Yehuda Kook calls the Holocaust an essential "medical" operation (like a painful but necessary amputation) for ending the exile and causing redemption to flourish (this is a quote from memory, because I do not have the books here). In short, these thoughts are always running around in my head when I wear my uniform, until some sergeant yells at me, "Come on, soldier, get that rifle up! We're moving out to the firing range!" So we've moved out, and now we're resting between drills, and I am taking advantage of my rest time to write you.

I was happy to read that you're not giving up on your year of service in Beit She'an. That's an opportunity for real giving, and I'm sure you'll feel happiness and satisfaction after this year. I imagine you will encounter more displays of suspicion and even hostility. Don't be put off by them. All the same, I suggest you approach the population you'll be working with not just as a giver, but as a receiver as well; not just as a teacher, but as a learner. I'm sure you will discover that you have a lot to learn even from people who hardly know how to read and write, but who possess rich life experience, a deep cultural tradition going back many years, and inner strengths which have withstood difficult tests, tests you cannot even imagine (compared to our parents, we all were raised with a silver spoon in our mouths). With such an approach I am sure you will discover that you have not only given but received an enormous amount. Be strong, and don't give up.

I'm being called to muster, so I've got to sign off.

Take care,

Dov

P.S. Our sphere of operations will be in the southern Sinai. We'll have a ball!

MARCH 15, 1973

Hi, Soldier!

Once again you've surprised me – twice, for that matter. First, that you wrote me already on the second day after induction. That's very nice of you and I appreciate it. Second, that in the middle of your training, instead of grabbing a little rest, you are thinking about faith and the Holocaust and the Jewish state, and even sharing all of your thoughts with me. With all your pondering, don't lose track of where you are and make stupid mistakes. Take care of yourself! Remember, you're in the army now and not in yeshiva among all the books.

How I envy you that you are going to be serving in the Sinai! The Sinai's amazing scenery and the stunning experiences from our trip there don't leave me. Make sure you get in some scuba diving off the Sinai coast. Don't miss a hike through the Santa Katarina area. Don't be lazy. Climb to the top of Jebel Musa.[1] In short, take advantage of this opportunity to have a bit of fun too.

It's simply amazing to discover how much you and my Bible teacher are exact opposites. For him, the Holocaust is resounding proof against faith. "How can one believe in God after the Holocaust?" he asks us, sort of rhetorically. "How can one believe in a God Who killed a million children in the Holocaust?" he repeats over and over. For him, the Holocaust is a sort of deathblow to the possibility of faith. For you, by contrast, the Holocaust actually strengthens faith, and you write about it as though it were some normal part of the process of a nation's establishment. There is something outrageous about your approach – are a million children a sort of springboard to our having a country? What kind of God is it Who kills six million Jews in order to fulfill His promise to establish a country for His people? Does that seem reasonable to you? Does that seem logical? One time you've got to see our Bible teacher in action. When he talks about the Holocaust, he gets filled with anger at God and the rabbis and the religious. It sometimes even frightens me a little. But I've got to say that I identify (regarding the Holocaust) with his anger and with his heresy much more than with your faith and resignation.

---

[1] "The Mountain of Moses" – Mount Sinai.

Since you're in the army now, I'll understand even if your answer is delayed. I'll be happy to read about your experiences. Take care of yourself, Soldier.

Take care,

Talia

SHUSHAN PURIM [MARCH 19, 1973], RAS SUDR

ב"ה

Dear Talia,

That's it. We've acclimated and started carrying out our missions. Our company has taken up positions along the Gulf of Suez – Abu Rudeis, Ras Sudr, A-Tur – and we're patrolling and guarding the area's vital installations. You must be aware that

At the wedding of the Barnoy-Shandur family, 1973

since the Six-Day War, large oil fields have been discovered in the Gulf of Suez. How much we have hoped and prayed to find a little oil in our tiny land! And now, together with the expanses of the Sinai, God has also given us this marvelous gift – oil reserves. The Egyptians were in the Sinai for many years, and nothing was discovered in this desolate wilderness. And now, the Jewish people arrived in the promised land, and wonderful treasures have been revealed. If only we will have the good sense to appreciate this marvelous gift and the strength to protect it. Right now we are carrying out this national mission and protecting the oil installations for the Jewish people.

Once a week, a company patrol goes out to the area of Santa Katarina, and I will be joining that patrol two weeks from now. I am waiting my turn with baited breath; your descriptions have really built up my appetite.

I'm happy that your Bible teacher is back in your letters. For me as well, he has become a very meaningful character, and I often find myself having imaginary debates with him. I too understand and even identify with your teacher's anger against God and the rabbis. Hagi told me that his father as well, whose family was lost in the Holocaust, is full of anger against the rabbis, who were opposed to making aliya to Israel before the Holocaust. (Hagi's father came to Israel before the Holocaust and is almost the only survivor from his family.) If you read my last letter to you carefully, you'll discover that I too think I would have a rough time remaining religious (and perhaps Jewish altogether) after the Holocaust, if not for the establishment of the state. Whoever was filled with doubts because of the Holocaust can suddenly, literally, see the revelation of the Divine Presence. After all, the state's establishment, and the fulfillment of the prophecies, and the Bible's words of solace are literally a divine revelation before our eyes. This revelation is so strong that it overcomes all the doubts aroused by the Holocaust.

When I returned with Hagi from our last meeting with you, we spoke about the Holocaust. Hagi mentioned an amazing midrash[1] about a verse in the book of Psalms. The midrash describes the redemption process via a story about a father and a son who were going on an arduous journey. The son asks the father: "Father, when will we come to the state?" (I'm quoting from memory because I don't have books with me), and his father gives him a surprising answer: "Son, when you see the cemetery, you'll know we are near the state." (I remember that I checked the midrash myself, and the terms "state"[2] and "cemetery" appear in the original.)

---

[1] Midrash Psalms, chapter 20, regarding the verse "May the Lord answer you in time of trouble."

[2] *Medina* in the Hebrew.

When I heard the midrash, my immediate reaction was, "Wait a second! That's the Holocaust, heralding the Jewish state's establishment." There's something terrible about this midrash, but also something that makes you happy and gives you strength. With all the difficulty in understanding the meaning of the connection between the Holocaust and the state, it turns out that these are two sides of the same coin – the redemption. It turns out that the great catastrophe is part of the divine plan, at the end of which is the complete redemption and the messianic era. Thus, this is one more prophecy that has been fulfilled, another forecast of our sages that has crystallized as a historic reality.

You know, Talia, that a lot of midrashim and rabbinic sources describe our age, the period of the start of the redemption (the "messianic footsteps," in the Talmud's words), as a period of religious, spiritual, and moral crisis, plagued by a profound generation gap, the rejection of faith, and the proliferation of heresy ("the government will become heretical... impudence will increase...the scholars' meeting place will be used for harlotry...children will not fear their parents...").[3] In short, there will be religious rebellion and moral chaos. All this will develop alongside a flourishing economy ("the vineyard will yield its fruit...").

Our sages said all of these things thousands of years ago. And in our own age, the age of the return to Zion and the ingathering of the exiles, the exact descriptions and scenarios of our sages are being played out. Is that not amazing? For someone who believes in the divine inspiration of our sages and the prophetic tradition they transmitted to us, the fulfillment of their forecasts is not surprising. And the Holocaust as well, ("the cemetery preceding the state") is part of those forecasts.

So even if I don't understand a thing, at least I can tell myself that all this terrible suffering that we have undergone is part of a great divine plan, intended to bring all of mankind to its goal, its purpose, its perfection. Can I tell you that

---

[3] Sanhedrin 97a, as well as the last mishna in Tractate Sota.

I understand these developments? No, I cannot. Can I tell you that the precise fulfillment of these developments foreseen by the prophets and sages of Israel strengthens my faith? Yes, that I can say.

Oops! Everyone is already in the jeep, waiting just for me to go out on the patrol.

Take care,

Dov

P.S. I wonder what your Bible teacher will say about all these midrashim. For sure, he will say that he is a Bible teacher, not a Midrash teacher. Don't let them give you evasive answers like that. I want to hear a serious answer from him.

MARCH 29, 1973

Dear Dov,

Your letter reminded me of our trip to the Sinai. I really miss the Sinai's scenery. In your patrol at Santa Katarina, make sure you take advantage of it to climb Jebel Musa. Don't miss scuba diving at Sharm. You'll have the time of your life there.

It's really amazing what you wrote about the connection, appearing already in the midrashim, between the Holocaust and the establishment of the state. It's hard to believe that things describing our period so precisely were written thousands of years ago. But you've got to explain to me why. What logic is there to that connection? I'm unwilling to accept your telling me, "That's what it says," period. True, it's worth a lot, because the fact that somebody foresaw this process so many years ago implies a plan, and every plan has its own logic. But you don't say a word about the logic of the plan. Who needs a Holocaust to establish a country? Is this the merciful, benevolent God that you believe in?

I also don't accept your relating to secular Jews as impudent people who don't honor their parents. (You quote the

112

midrashim that speak of "increased impudence...children not honoring their parents," and all sorts of other slurs against us.) In every family there are arguments and tensions between parents and children, but I don't think this characterizes only our times. Such is human nature, and I imagine the situation has always existed. I don't think we are better than previous generations, but I also don't think we're worse. Sometimes I think you tend to treat us, the secular, with scorn, to relate to us with generalizations based more on your prejudices than on the reality and the facts.

Perhaps you forget, but I will remind you: The members of the kibbutzim and moshavim are at the forefront of the IDF's combat units; they head the settlements in the Sinai, the Golan Heights, and the Jordan Valley. They are leaders in volunteering in border towns and development towns. And you know what? We, the secular, are even leaders in the Bible. Hagi told us that he was the winner of the Bible contest for youth when he was still studying in a secular school and hadn't yet become religious. Most of the participants and winners in Bible contests are from secular schools.

So please, don't make fun of us.

Awaiting your response,

Talia

ב"ה

8 Nisan 5733 [April 10, 1973], Ras Sudr

Dear Talia,

Just this second I heard on the radio about the liquidation of the master terrorists in Beirut.[1] How proud and happy I am! How thankful I am to God to be living in a generation in which

---

[1] On the night of April 9, 1973, an Israeli commando unit, headed by Ehud Barak, liquidated a number of PLO leaders in Beirut in retaliation for the Munich massacre of Israeli sportsmen on September 5, 1972.

Jewish blood is not cheap! Today, matters came full circle. Half a year ago, abominable terrorists killed our eleven sportsmen in Germany, and now the day of vengeance has arrived. They didn't get away with it this time. Jewish blood has a price.

Always at times like this, my thoughts wander to my parents' families, the grandparents, uncles, and aunts murdered in the Holocaust as though they were cockroaches or flies. Their lives were considered worthless in the eyes of the nations. Not only did the Germans slaughter them, but all the nations of Europe willingly and joyfully collaborated in the genocide of our people. And whoever did not collaborate stood on the side and was silent, usually throwing in a little wink for good measure. Not a bomb was dropped on Auschwitz over the five years of the Jews' annihilation, even though thousands of tons of bombs were dropped on the German factory that stood next to it.

Consider to what depths the Jewish people had fallen, how low they were, just one generation ago. And here we have been privileged, with God's help, to rise up from the ashes, to establish a glorious state and army, and to restore self-worth and dignity to the life of a Jew. Once more our lives are precious, and whoever strikes us will be struck a hundredfold in return.

In his article, "My Beloved Knocks" (which I believe I have already mentioned in previous letters), Rabbi Soloveitchik writes that the State of Israel is entitled to interpret the biblical commands of "an eye for an eye" literally and not just to take revenge according to a ratio of one to one, but according to a ratio of a thousand to one – a thousand eyes in exchange for one Jewish eye. He is a proud Jew (I'm sorry we have not been privileged to have him live with us in Israel).

You rightly ask: But where is the logic, where is the justice in the terrible tragedy that befell the Jewish people during the Holocaust? I want to share with you my thoughts that occurred to me after I read the letters of Rabbi Abraham Isaac Kook to the Jews of the Diaspora. He lived in Israel before the Holocaust, and in dozens of letters he beseeched the Jews of the exile to move to Israel to save themselves. You know what? He wasn't the only one and he wasn't the first. A hundred years before him, there rose up the greatest of the sages of Lithuania, Rabbi Elijah of Vilna[2] and asked his disciples to move to Israel, because the time of redemption had arrived. In our yeshiva, we've got a little book called *Kol HaTor* [The voice of the turtledove], written by one of those disciples who moved to Israel. There he tells how the Gra begged his students to move to Israel, warning them of the destruction awaiting anyone who stayed in the exile. And indeed, a few of his disciples move to Israel and settled in Tzfat, and afterwards in Jerusalem, but the Jewish masses remained in the exile. (Hagi is seventh generation in the land. He is a descendant of one of the disciples of the Gra who came to Israel about 150 years ago). After the Gra, important rabbis appeared, "heralds of Zionism," Rabbi Kalischer, Rabbi Alkalai, Rabbi Guttmacher, and others, and they too called upon the Jewish people to come to Israel. A few, really just a handful, responded, but the masses remained in Europe.

After them rose the rabbis of Hibbat Tzion[3] [Love of Zion], among them great Torah sages of European Jewry like Rabbi Naftali Tzvi Yehuda Berlin, the Netziv of Volozhin, the head of the Volozhin Yeshiva, "mother of all yeshivas" in eastern Europe. They too called upon the Jewish people to move to Israel, because the time of redemption had arrived, and once again, only a few responded (the founders of the first colonies of the First Aliya).[4] The Jewish masses remained in the exile. And then Herzl emerged and the Zionist Organization was

---

[2] Known as the Gra, short for HaGaon Rabbi Eliyahu (the illustrious Rabbi Elijah).

[3] Also known as Hovevei Tzion, Hibbat Tzion was a movement that included groups formed in eastern Europe in the 1880s to promote Jewish immigration to the land of Israel and to advance Jewish settlement there, particularly agricultural. These groups are now considered the forerunners of modern Zionism.

[4] The First Aliya refers to the first large wave of Zionist immigration to the land of Israel, between 1882 until 1903. The immigrants were mostly from eastern Europe and Yemen.

founded and with it, the practical possibilities of moving to Israel increased and expanded.

Once again, prominent rabbis like Rabbi Kook and Rabbi Reines emerged, calling upon the Jewish people to move to Israel. And once again, the masses remained in Europe. And then a miracle occurred. After the First World War, Britain, which had conquered the land of Israel, recognized the right of the Jewish people to establish "a national home in Palestine." Following the British, all the nations of the world, which had joined together in the League of Nations, recognized the right of the Jewish people to the land of Israel and charged England with the "mandate" of helping the Jewish people to establish their national home here. Once again, Rabbi Kook, together with prominent rabbis in Eretz Yisrael such as Rabbi Uziel,[5] called upon the Jewish people to take advantage of the historic opportunity and to move to Israel. And once again, the Jewish masses, including the haredim, remained apathetic and hostile to the great miracles, to the dramatic change that has taken place with the Balfour Declaration.[6]

For 150 years, God had been trying to budge the Jewish people out of the exile. He sent faithful emissaries. He worked miracles and wonders (consider what an amazing miracle it is that suddenly all the nations recognized our right to the land of Israel), and the Jewish people remained apathetic. If the Jews were not ready to liquidate the exile of their own free will, apparently God had no choice but to do it in a harsh, painful, and cruel manner (the "amputation" that Rabbi Tzvi Yehuda Kook spoke about). "I will reign over you with a strong hand, and with an outstretched arm, and with overflowing fury" [Ezekiel 20:33]. And the fact is that it worked. Suddenly, after the

---

[5] Rabbi Ben-Zion Meir Hai Uziel (1880–1953) was the Sephardic chief rabbi of the British Mandate of Palestine from 1939 to 1948 and of Israel from 1948 until 1953. He was a close friend of Rabbi Abraham Isaac Kook.

[6] The Balfour Declaration was a letter written on November 2, 1917, by British Foreign Secretary Arthur James Balfour to Lord Rothschild making public Great Britain's support for a Jewish homeland in Palestine. The document led the League of Nations to entrust the United Kingdom with the Palestine Mandate in 1922.

Holocaust, the entire Jewish people became Zionist; even the Reformed Jews, who were anti-Zionists until the Holocaust, became part of the Zionist movement. Even haredi Jewry, which was mostly anti-Zionist, was forced to reestablish its Torah centers and yeshivot in Eretz Yisrael, and today Eretz Yisrael is the greatest Torah center in the world.

The Zionist movement itself was shaken up after the Holocaust, setting for itself a clear goal of establishing a state, and (when Britain reneged on its mandate to help establish the Jewish homeland) it went to war against the British Empire and succeeded in banishing the British from the land. In short, all these processes happened after the Holocaust, and, to a large degree, under the influence of the Holocaust. And that was it – the end of the European exile, and the start of Jewish independence in Eretz Yisrael.

Even the American exile is being finished off, albeit by way of "the quiet Holocaust" – assimilation and mixed marriages, which are wiping out the Jewish community in America at a rate of at least 1 million Jews every 10 years.[7] And once more, unfortunately, only a few Jews are moving here from America, but they are privileged to be partners with us in the redemption process instead of being part of something that is shrinking and being wiped out in America.

I know I am writing you some very harsh things. I avoid voicing them even among my friends in yeshiva. But you ask and demand an answer, so I'm letting you in on my thoughts about the Holocaust in the most candid, open manner. As you recall, we promised to be honest with each other.

In the book *Kol HaTor* by Rabbi Yisrael of Shklov (a disciple of the Gra), a shocking story is told. He tells about the Gra, who one Shabbat broke out in bitter weeping after the reading of the Torah and the haftara (every Shabbat at synagogue services, we chant a section from the Torah and a chapter from the Prophets, called the haftara). When he had composed himself,

---

[7] As of the year 2000, the assimilation rate in the United States was between 50 percent and 52 percent.

he showed his disciples the verse from the book of Obadiah, which had been read that Shabbat – "on Zion's mount a remnant shall survive" [1:17]. Whoever remains in the exile, said the Gra to his disciples, shall be annihilated. Only in Eretz Yisrael, on Mount Zion, shall a remnant of the Jewish people survive, and from that shall spring forth the complete redemption. This story has been accompanying me since I read that book, and every time I say goodbye to the yeshiva students who came from abroad for a year of study in Israel, I tell them this story.

We are so lucky! We are so lucky that we live in a generation that is the last of servitude to the nations and the first of redemption. How fortunate we are that we are privileged to be soldiers in the IDF, which defends the lives of Jews in Israel and throughout the world. How fortunate that we are privileged to learn the Torah of Eretz Yisrael in happiness and joy. And how fortunate we are...that I'm now being called to my turn at guard duty.

So take care,

Dov

❖ ❖ ❖

ב"ה

THE DAY AFTER PESACH [APRIL 24, 1973], RAS SUDR

Dear Talia,

I haven't yet received a letter from you, but I'm writing you again anyway. I want to share with you one of the greatest experiences of my whole life – Pesach on Mount Sinai. This was the most exciting Pesach of my life.

Before the holiday they asked our unit for volunteers to do guard duty in a secret army communications installation. After hesitating briefly, I volunteered. It turned out that the installation was on a mountain, Jebel Katarina (next to Jebel Musa). Every stint of guard duty at the installation lasts a whole week, since just climbing the mountain takes half a day (there is no road there, only a path, and the climb is on foot). We traveled to the Santa Katarina monastery, which is at the foot of the mountain, through Wadi Piran. You were absolutely right. This is an amazing wadi with charming desert scenery. We stopped for a short while in a Bedouin encampment, and they offered us (very sweet) tea, as well as all sorts of traditional dishes (which obviously, for *kashrut* reasons, I didn't touch). Everything all around looked exactly like in the days of our ancestors when they left Egypt – goatskin tents, water drawn from a large cistern in the courtyard, a caravan of camels, a flock of sheep by the water trough, people gathered in the shade of the palm trees...

In short, it was as though the Bible had come alive. We would have stayed there more and more, but our commander hurried us on so that we would manage to reach the monastery before dark.

Next to the monastery is a small military camp. There we slept the night, and the next morning we set out with a Bedouin guide to the top of the mountain. Our knapsacks were carried by a camel that walked with the guide. The higher we climbed (the climb lasted about four hours), the more short of breath we became, but the scenery became more and more spectacular. Jebel Katarina is a bit higher than Jebel Musa, and its altitude is about 2,000 meters [6,500 feet].

Slowly the whole Sinai expanse opened up before us – the blue Gulf of Suez on the distant horizon, the desert oases and oil installations along the coast, and the mountains climbing ever upward toward the peak of Jebel Katarina. Had it been up to me, I would've stopped every five minutes to look at the spectacular scenery, but our platoon commander hurried us along so that we'd make it before the intense midday heat.

We arrived in the afternoon, several hours before it was time for *bedikat hametz*, the yearly, pre-Pesach ritual of looking for *hametz* [leavened foods, forbidden on Passover]. We had no choice. Whoever was not on guard duty or manning the radio was enlisted to make the kitchen kosher for Pesach (it looked terribly neglected). It was just our luck that all of us were skilled at making kitchens kosher, since the previous year we had all participated in making army kitchens kosher for Pesach (let's see if you remember where I was). We finished working at almost midnight, and then I had to start...my guard duty. I asked to do my guard duty outside, because if I manned the radio inside the installation, I was sure I would fall asleep. Sure enough, the cold mountain air kept me awake. Only as morning was approaching did I go to sleep for several hours (a friend switched with me just before my time was up, moments before I almost collapsed from tiredness).

Talia, you can well imagine that celebrating the Pesach Seder at a spot looking out on the Red Sea and the Sinai expanses is a special experience. The whole Seder night I felt "as though I, personally, had gone forth from Egypt."[1] In the middle of the Seder I had a brief stint of guard duty – on the horizon you could see the lights from ships on the Red Sea, and with a bit of imagination you could see "the children of Israel crossing on dry land within the sea...with the water as a wall to their right and their left."

I came back to the dining room shack and I sang the songs of the Exodus with greater joy and gratitude to God than I had ever felt in all my life. What a privilege it is to live in a generation in which the Jewish people have returned to the expanses of the Sinai and can see the divine promise fulfilled: "I will set your borders from the Sea of Reeds to the Sea of Philistia, and from the wilderness to the Euphrates" [Exodus 23:31]. I pinched myself to be sure that I wasn't dreaming, that everything was really happening, that I was celebrating the Seder night as an IDF soldier atop Mount Sinai. And indeed, it was no dream. It is no illusion. And suddenly, in mid-Seder, I began to sing the song that expressed what I felt:

> It is no dream, my friend, it is no dream, my friend,
> No legend, if you will.

---

[1] This is a reference to the idea expressed in the Pesach Haggadah, a book of readings for the Passover Seder, that on Pesach each Jew should feel as if he himself were redeemed from the Egyptian bondage.

Because at Mount Sinai,
Because at Mount Sinai,
The bush is burning
Still.

All the guys yelled at me, "Hey! Have you gone nuts? What happened to you?" but I persevered, and in the end they all joined in. At the last line, "The tale shall be told of the return of the nation / back to the Sinai Revelation," the walls of the shack were trembling. I literally had a feeling of being at the Sinai Revelation, of the Divine Presence being revealed. Could there be a greater revelation of the *Shechina* (the Divine Presence) than the return to Zion in our day, and the fulfillment of the divine promise to the Jewish people after two thousand years of exile?

The next day I hiked a bit on the mountaintop (within the Shabbat walking boundary,[2] which is about a kilometer from the camp in every direction). I came upon an enormous cliff, a sort of shelf sticking out from the mountain, with an abyss below it of hundreds of meters. At the bottom, at the foot of the mountain, an enormous valley stretched forth, the drainage basin of Wadi Piran.

Suddenly before my eyes appeared the image of Moses. Maybe he was really standing there, on that rock ("See, there is a place near Me. Station yourself on the rock" – Exodus 34:21). Below him, in the valley, were all the Israelites, arranged in camps by tribe and family. Perhaps here, for the first time, he gave voice to the cry that has accompanied us for thousands of years: "Hear, O Israel! The Lord is our God! The Lord is one!" Following Moses' cry, the people's thunderous voice resounded, the mountains trembled, and a new chapter in the history of mankind began. Perhaps it was here that the people stood, millions of men, women, and children, with God revealing Himself to His people, and letting them hear the Ten Commandments:

---

2 This refers to the prohibition of *tehum Shabbat*, which forbids traveling a certain distance outside one's city of residence on the Sabbath.

"I am the Lord your God…" The loud sound of the strong wind blowing upon the mountain suddenly sang to me the verses of the Ten Commandments: "…Who has taken you out of the land of Egypt and the house of bondage." I stood there on the cliff, deep in thought for so long that they began to worry about me. They sent somebody to look for me, and when we arrived back in the camp, we sang the verses from the Song of Deborah which talk about the Sinai Revelation: "O Lord, when You came forth from Seir, advanced from the country of Edom, the earth trembled, the heavens dripped. Yea, the clouds dripped water. The mountains quaked, before the Lord, Him of Sinai; before the Lord, God of Israel" [Judges 5:4–5].

That entire week on the mountain I was literally drunk, drunk from the scenery, from the sights, from the ancient sounds coming to life. The verses of the Ten Commandments and of "Hear O Israel" thundered in my ears all week long.

The return to Ras Sudr and routine really took a toll on me. It wasn't just the physical descent from the high mountains. It was the descent from the holy to the mundane.

This letter is a sort of last release over the marvelous experience of a week atop Mount Sinai. It was the most exciting Pesach of my life, and perhaps it will never return.

And how annoying it is to hear once more the cry: Dov! The patrol is leaving! They're all waiting for you! So I've got to sign off.

Take care,

Dov

MAY 1, 1973

Dear Soldier,

It turns out that you're not just a soldier, and not just a yeshiva student. You're also a poet! Your last letter was truly the work of a poet. How I envy you, that you live the Bible, that you see the Exodus and hear the Ten Commandments. When I was on

Mount Sinai, I was just plain tired and irritated over some old warts that bothered me as I walked. I'd be interested to know what you thought about the geological layers of Mount Sinai. When we were at Wadi Piran, they showed us in the walls of the Wadi the ancient layers that straddle the mountains. Each layer reflects millions of years of the world's development. How is that compatible for you with Genesis, which talks of six days of Creation? For us on our hikes, the whole thing became a real joke, with everyone trying to remember the name and age of every layer. The layers have such funny names – Mesozoic and things like that. Everyone was splitting their sides, adding in billions of years. As a religious person, how do you feel about all of those numbers and theories?

In our biology exam, there's a chapter on the theory of evolution. How do you deal with Darwin's theory, which talks of man's developing from a monkey? Our biology teacher told us that the religious are opposed to this theory because it contradicts the Bible. What's your opinion on this?

While you're having a blast on Mount Sinai, I've been having a blast with my practice matriculation exams, reciting mathematical formulas and historical dates. Those exams are so aggravating. To prepare for them, we devour humongous amounts of knowledge and facts, and I am sure that nothing will remain in my head from it the moment after the test. A lot of boys, and some girls as well, have said no thanks to this nightmare in advance, and they are working on the kibbutz at all sorts of jobs, and are really happy. Sometimes I'm sorry I didn't do the same. With all the pressure of those exams, I sometimes pick up your letters, and they carry me off to another world – serious, adult, interesting. I pray those exams will soon be behind me.

So keep sending me such beautiful letters. It really saves me.

Take care,

Talia

ב"ה

6 IYAR 5733 [MAY 8, 1973], RAS SUDR

Dear Talia,

Yesterday we managed to watch the Independence Day parade on TV.[1]

I was sorry I wasn't there, but even watching it on TV was a real experience. I remember the parades that were broadcast on the radio. We heard the broadcasters describing the tanks and the jets, and you needed a lot of imagination to guess how they looked. On TV, everything is real, as though you were there. It provides a bit of solace over our being so far from home (I haven't had a leave in three weeks).

Before I left for the army, I read an excellent book, which answers your questions in a very logical, organized fashion. It is called *Judaism and Evolution* by Avraham Korman. It's worth reading if you can get your hands on it (otherwise, God willing, I'll send it to you when I come back to yeshiva at the end of the year). There you'll find a lot of commentators interpreting the concept of six days of Creation to mean six ages, six eons. After all, man had not yet been created, so human concepts are not yet relevant. The six days are six periods of time, each of which could be millions of years, during which the world was created gradually, in stages.

Interestingly, both the Torah and contemporary science think the world was not created in its complete form all at once, but via a gradual process involving different stages. Korman quotes religious men of science who point to the parallelism between the stages described in Genesis and the stages of the world's development according to the theory of evolution. Light, the primal energy source, was created on the first day (or, in the language of science, in the first stage). The organization

---

[1] On Independence Day in 1973, the IDF held its last military parade, in which all the new weaponry with which Israel equipped itself after the Six-Day War was displayed.

of the continents and oceans took place on the second day. Plant life appeared on the third day. Life appeared on the fifth day – the fish and fowl, crawling and creeping creatures. All of that was the lower orders of life. The higher orders of life – the mammals – appeared only on the sixth day, and at the end of the sixth day, i.e., at the end of the process of biological creation, man appeared.

The general structure of the process described in the Torah exactly parallels the world's development according to the theory of evolution. The appearance of the orbs of light on the fourth day reflects a stage in which the atmosphere had become clear enough for the heavenly bodies, which determine the calendar, to be seen from Earth (Rashi on the Torah emphasizes that those bodies were created already on the first day, but appeared only on the fourth day). Korman emphasizes that in all the ancient Creation narratives, none depicts Creation as a gradual process other than that of Genesis. It turns out that the Torah preceded science by several thousand years.

The main difference between the scientific approach and that of the Bible is not about there being long periods and different stages, but rather one basic question: Did the various stages of the world's development (inanimate objects, plant life, animals, and man) appear mechanically (what science calls natural development), or did a higher power, a divine force, accompany the process and make it possible? Do you truly believe that without a higher power such a beautiful, orderly, and sophisticated world could have developed, a world of which so far we understand only a minuscule portion? (For example, what do we know about the mysteries of the human brain? Or the complexities of heredity and genes?)

Even regarding what we don't understand, we assume it operates according to set, well-planned laws, and every advance in any sphere of science does indeed confirm this assumption. Einstein, the greatest scientist in human history (a Jew, obviously, and even an active Zionist), once said, "God does not play dice with the universe." By this he meant that none of the universe is left up to chaos or disorder. Everything operates in a precise manner according to set laws, with a clear purpose, which can be expressed via mathematical formulas. By the way, several years ago I found in the National Library a small booklet by Einstein called *My World*. There he describes how precisely his scientific research brought him to faith in the existence of a higher power that created the cosmos. Without such faith, says Einstein, it is impossible to understand a thing. It's worth your reading the book.

I don't have any problem either, with evolution, which talks about man's developing from a monkey. After all, the Torah says, man has two dimensions, body and soul. I have no problem viewing the body as a continuation and development of the body of animals that are similar to man, like monkeys. The novel point of the Torah is precisely the dimension of the soul, which the Torah calls "the divine image." This is a dimension, unique to man, which has not developed from the animals, but which was granted to man as a new creation, enabling man to be a thinking, speaking being, one that understands and creates. Man has the ability to develop science and technology, philosophy and morality, literature and art, religion and faith. Also the scientific theories don't actually know how to explain the great spurts in the evolutionary process: from inanimate to plant, from plant to animal, from animal to man. The Torah calls these spurts "creation," since without the intervention of a higher power, it is impossible to understand them. Each such spurt takes place on a different day of the six days of Creation, since it expresses a new stage in the world's development.

You'll probably laugh at me, but the following really happened: I remember myself solving problems in physics and chemistry and exclaiming to myself, "How glorious Your works, O Lord!" [Psalms 104:24]. After all, the fundamental assumption of every solution is that laws of nature exist that can be expressed via mathematical formulas, and that the world operates according to these laws in a precise manner. Therefore, every stone, for example, falls to earth in accordance with those same laws of gravity. Then, we need only add in the special conditions applying to each situation (mass, altitude, momentum, etc.) and obtain a result, which will be correct for all cases in which those conditions apply. Isn't that amazing? Could anyone think that it's all a coincidence? That it works out by itself? That it happens automatically?

Forgive my using a vulgar expression: You'd have to be an idiot to think that. No, I don't think everyone who does not believe in God is an idiot, but something seems really crazy to me about thinking that everything happens by chance. Whoever replaces "God" [Elokim] with "nature,"[2] out of a belief that everything is arbitrary and coincidental, and that there is no divine force that created and directs this entire, marvelous system, is simply... (It would be unseemly for me to repeat myself.)

In short, you should realize that all the stories they tell you about a substantial, unsolvable contradiction between religion and science consist more of unfounded prejudices than of a correct, precise description of the reality. Today there are many hundreds of religious men of science in the universities and the research institutes in Israel and throughout the world. At Bar-Ilan University, which is a religious university, there are religious men of science in all the faculties and spheres of research.

I don't want you to get the impression from me that there are no difficulties and no contradictions and no problems between the two worlds – Torah and faith on the one hand, and science and research on the other. One has to deal bravely and honestly with the problems in order to advance serious solutions. Yet it is presently clear that the day is past when it seemed as though a religious person could not work in science, and that a man of science could not be a believer and observant.

---

[2] The reference is to *gematria*, a system in Judaism which assigns numerical values to letters, words, and phrases, in the belief that words or phrases sharing the same numerical value bear some relation to each other. Here, the Hebrew word for "God," Elokim, and the Hebrew word for "nature," *teva*, both have the numerical value 86.

According to science...it is presently 11:50 at night (or, more precisely, 23:50), and in ten minutes I've got to report for guard duty. So I'm going to get myself organized with my gun and equipment so I can take over the previous watch on time.

I didn't have a chance to sleep before this watch, but believe me, the hours I write to you (and read your letters) give me a lot of strength.

So good night,

Take care,

Dov

MAY 18, 1973

Dear Dov,

You sometimes surprise me with your lack of tolerance toward anyone who does not think like you. You explain your beliefs and worldview well, but you really mock whoever does not share your views. Can you really call my history teacher or my biology teacher an idiot, since both of them say they don't believe in God? Don't you think you're exaggerating? You can say that they are mistaken, that they don't understand certain things, that they are not looking at the whole picture, etc. etc. But why use such insulting, hurtful expressions?

I personally very much identify with what you say, that it cannot be that the world could function without a higher force having created it and directing it. That seems very logical to me, and motivated by this faith I even sometimes pray and ask God for all sorts of things. But unlike you, I do not mock all the people around me who are atheists and don't believe in God at all.

You know what, Dov? Every time I see the soldiers from the kibbutz, who serve at least three years in the army, and most of them sign up for another year or two in the standing army, I think of you. It hurts me that you don't serve three full years the way they do, and with all of your Zionistic ideals you put in half service instead of full service. You cannot imagine how much this bothers me that you do less than others although you speak so enthusiastically about the army and about the Jewish state. Sometimes I feel like telling you that if you want to be an honest person, at peace with himself, you owe it to yourself to give full service without tricks. In all sorts of debates on my kibbutz, I want to tell people that there are yeshiva students who serve in the army, but I hold back, because I would have to admit that even they only give half service and not full service.

I know I am tormenting you on this point, so I will stop here. Don't miss scuba diving at Sharm el-Sheikh when you get the chance.

Take care,

Talia

ב"ה

26 Iyar 5733 [May 28, 1973], Ras Sudr

Dear Talia,

You're so right! It's forbidden for me to use insulting expressions regarding people who don't think like me. I tell myself that all the time, and I also try to work to improve myself. The truth is that when people are debating God and faith, it sometimes aggravates me, because God's existence is so clear to me. God is as present for me as the rifle lying by my side. If someone comes and says, regarding an object that you see with your own eyes, that he doesn't see a thing, you'll get upset with him and start looking for what is messed up about him that prevents him from seeing something whose existence is so clear and obvious.

You don't know how much I too am bothered by the thought that one has to give full army service without any tricks. You are right that Torah Jews have to provide an example

129

for others through their personal behavior. My struggle over this matter never gives me rest. Yet, all in all, I do not regret the track I chose, which combines Torah with the army.

Life is complex, and there are a lot of values and ideals and ambitions and dreams that we want to fulfill. When you've got a lot of ideals, you have no choice but to find a way to integrate them. Any integration will harm the complete fulfillment of any one ideal per se, but ultimately you'll attain something fuller and more complete. After all, the soldiers from your kibbutz, who serve three years or four years, don't learn Torah, and the yeshiva students, who don't serve in the army, learn more Torah than I do. Seemingly, I've got every reason in the world to feel inferior to both groups. I also have good reason to feel inferior to those who only study in university and advance in science and research.

Yet I am seeking a way to integrate all the ideals – Torah learning (which I strive to invest my greatest efforts in) together with general knowledge (which I am continuing to progress in, even following my matriculation exams) and military service (which I am trying to make as combat-oriented as possible). Obviously, I also intend to add to these three ideals, establishing a family (hopefully soon), settling Eretz Yisrael (perhaps a religious settlement on the Golan Heights), and being involved in Jewish and Zionist education (perhaps as a teacher of religious or secular subjects). In short, it is clear to me that if someone adopts one ideal and devotes himself to it entirely, he will achieve greater things in that sphere than someone who strives to integrate different ideals. Yet I still feel that there is greater spiritual and ethical perfection and greater closeness to God among those who integrate and combine the different worlds. I believe that in this matter I am following the path of Rabbi Kook (you certainly know who he is by now), who longed to combine and unite the different streams and forces that exist within the Jewish people.

How happy Rabbi Kook would have been had he been privileged to see the great victory of the Jewish people in the

Six-Day War! For me, the biggest holiday of the year is not June 5, 28 Iyar on the Hebrew calendar, the day Jerusalem was liberated in 1967, but two days before, June 3, 26 Iyar, today's date, the day I am writing this letter. It is hard to believe, but it was no dream. Within three hours on June 3, 1967, the first day of the war, our air force destroyed the air forces of four countries: Egypt, Syria, Jordan, and Iraq. It's just unbelievable! What miracles we were privileged to see with our own eyes! Motti Hod, the commander of the air force during the Six-Day War, related that he too did not believe the reports by the pilots who returned from the impossible missions that they had been charged with. Almost all of the jets returned home safely, and all of them carried out their missions completely. In three hours, and not in six days (although that too would have been a great miracle), we vanquished the four Arab countries that had planned to attack us.

During those hours, I was in the bomb shelter of the Netiv Meir yeshiva high school in Jerusalem, full of fear and foreboding. Outside, bombs were exploding, launched by Jordanian cannons at Jerusalem. Over the radio, we heard the pronouncements of the Arab radio stations (such as The Voice of Thunder from Cairo), declaring that Tel Aviv had been conquered and was burning down. We were really frightened, and only the head of our yeshiva, Rabbi Arye Bina, circulated among us, full of faith and hope, offering all of us encouragement. I do not know where he drew his faith that ultimately all would end well, with a great victory. Only in the afternoon did we start to hear rumors that the radio stations of the world were reporting the destruction of the air forces of all the Arab countries. We were really in seventh heaven. In Aramaic you say, "From a deep pit to a high mountain."

The feeling of joy and gratitude that filled me during those moments when the true picture of the great victory began to become clear, that feeling has been with me since the war. Every year on 26 Iyar, the first day of the Six-Day War, I dress in Shabbat finery and recite the Hallel prayer of thanks to God. Since the Chief Rabbinate established 28 Iyar, the day Jerusalem was liberated, as the day on which Hallel is to be recited, I therefore make do with reciting the psalms of the Hallel prayer [Psalms 113–119] without a blessing. If it were up to me, I would establish a six-day holiday, and not a one-day holiday. Each day of the Six-Day War we conquered another area of Eretz Yisrael through open miracles. On the first day we conquered the Gaza Strip. On the second day we conquered Samaria. On the third day we conquered Jerusalem. On the fourth day we conquered the Sinai and the hills of Hebron. On the fifth day we conquered the Jordan Valley. On the sixth day we conquered the Golan Heights. It's like the six days of Creation, in which every day something new was created.

How fortunate we are to have been privileged to live in this generation. How fortunate we are that we are privileged to serve in the army. How fortunate we are that we are privileged to guard the shores of the Red Sea at the foot of Mount Sinai... Wow! The night is really dark, and it's quite frightening to go out to my guard duty. It's more pleasant to guard on moonlit nights. Yet we've got an apparatus for night vision at our post (using starlight), and that makes you feel a lot better.

So have a happy Jerusalem Day,

Be well,

Dov

JUNE 7, 1973

Dear Dov,

Right now, everyone is deep in matriculation exams and there's literally no time to breathe. I hope you appreciate the fact that despite the great pressure, I am writing you. I know you are happy to receive my letters there in the far-off Sinai, so for you I am willing to make the effort. It's hard to believe how much pressure there is. My head is full of numbers and dates and formulas and names and verses, and everything is mixing together into a big sort of salad in which it's hard to distinguish between math and history. I am waiting sooooo anxiously for the moment when we will be after the last exam – a mighty screech will burst forth and echo throughout the kibbutz: Enough! It's over! Just as for you the song about the Sinai Revelation constantly echoes in your brain, for me, the song that echoes in my brain all the time is: Let out a roar! It's all over. Enough! I just want sooooo bad for those tests to be behind me, so we can breathe again, read a good book, sit with friends and chat over a cup of coffee. How were *your* matriculation exams? Did you get so tensed up you couldn't breathe, like what happened to me?

Beyond the horizon of the matriculation exams my trip to Sinai approaches. We are organizing ourselves for a two-week trip to Sinai with a scuba diving course at Sharm el-Sheikh. I really get excited when we talk about the trip. I remember the wonderful scuba diving we did in the Sinai last year, and I just can't wait. This time, the Sinai has something it didn't have last year – a soldier – whom I'm dying to see. This time I'm not giving in. If you won't come to Sharm el-Sheikh (where we will be most of the time), then I will look for you in the Sinai.

Yesterday we had our celebration of the first fruits. All the preschool and elementary school children did a procession with little baskets with samples of all the fruits grown on the kibbutz. All the children were decorated with flower wreaths on their heads, and boy, did they look funny! All the baskets were presented to the representative of the Jewish National Fund, who made some sort of silly speech about the redemption of the land and the redemption of the nation. There were a whole lot of guests and parents of members who got really excited and clapped their hands the whole time.

Maya stood by me and got really aggravated by the whole thing. It angered her that they go through the whole first fruits ceremony without mentioning the Temple or the *kohanim* and *levi'im*. After all, in biblical times they brought the first fruits to the Temple, and the Jewish National Fund is not the Temple. When you get down to it, the JNF is just a company to purchase land and encourage settlement. Our Bible teacher was standing not far from us, and Maya decided to talk to him about what got her mad in the ceremony. She was sure he would support her, since he's a Bible teacher. It turned out she was wrong. He went into a long explanation about how redeeming the lands of Eretz Yisrael and settling them with Jews was just like building the Temple. It was even more than that, he said, because as long as Jews only dreamed about the Temple, they remained in the exile and didn't do a thing. Yet when the pioneers began talking about redeeming the soil of Eretz Yisrael, settlement began and aliya began, and the state came into being. Nothing came of all the talk about the Temple, but a Jewish state emerged from talk about the land.

Maya was quite surprised by this whole speech (which I actually really liked). She got aggravated with the Bible teacher as well, and some sort of line slipped out like, "You're babbling nonsense" (I didn't hear it exactly). She got really confused and didn't stop apologizing, but when all is said and done, she disagreed with him. If we don't keep praying for the Temple, and if we substitute land purchase for it – so she argued – then in the end we won't have land either.

Maya is yelling at me now that from all my letter writing I'll fail all my exams. So it's back to the rat race. Take care of yourself, Soldier. I really want to see you.

Talia

ב"ה

22 Sivan 5733 [June 22, 1973], Ras Sudr

Dear Talia,

I actually think Maya is right and not your teacher. You know what? I think the poet Haim Hefer also thinks Maya is right. You must be asking yourself what Haim Hefer has to do with any of this. So listen to a story:

We did our basic training at Camp 80 near Pardes Hanna. In that army camp there was a memorial room dedicated to soldiers from the Nahal Infantry Brigade, and besides pictures of a lot of soldiers there was a little library there. When we had a free moment (mostly on Shabbat, because during the week they kept us going all the time), I would go into their library to read and to browse through books. I found a wonderful book there, which I kept coming back to. It was a book of poetry by Haim Hefer called *Soldiers' Muster*. It contains poems he wrote during the Six-Day War, and every one of them is more beautiful and more moving than the next. I was especially impressed by two poems – "We Were as Dreamers" and "The Paratroopers Weep," which I copied into my notebook (I've got a little note-

During army service at Ras Sudr, Sharm el-Sheikh, 1973. Right, Dov; left, Rabbi Haim Sabato.

book into which I copy Torah thoughts I want to memorize, or nice poems that I like, and all sorts of other neat things). These two poems by Haim Hefer share a common motif – that it was the Temple that gave the Jewish people the strength through the generations, and in our own generation as well. Listen to what he writes in his poem "We Were as Dreamers":

> Alongside the fighters of the Six-Day War
> Marched those who had valiantly fought before

The formidable warriors of '48
And those hanged by the British during the Mandate
And the fallen heroes of the underground
All singing a song, so moving! So profound!
"Soon in our day! May the Temple be rebuilt!"
We breached that wall! We fought to the hilt!
The Temple Mount was ours! We had done our part!
Spurred on by their song, which burns in our heart.

This is a really amazing song which says in the strongest way possible: The prayer, and dreams about the Temple are the source of strength, even of the soldiers who conquered Jerusalem in our day. Without those prayers, without the dreams of Jerusalem and of the Temple, not only would we not have returned to Eretz Yisrael, but we would long ago have disappeared. Your Bible teacher makes light of the very thing responsible for his having come to Eretz Yisrael in the first place.

There is another marvelous poem by Haim Hefer – "The Paratroopers Weep" – where once more he expresses that same sense of connection between the generations.

This wall saw them tired and worn
Wounded and torn,
Rushing toward this wall
In shock, shouting or silent,
Leaping through the Old City alleyways
Like madmen
Caked in dust with cracked lips
And whispering:
If I forget thee!
If I forget thee, O Jerusalem...

How right he is! Surely, without that dream about Jerusalem – "For out of Zion shall the Torah go forth, and the word of God from Jerusalem" – it would not have been worth it to suffer for two thousand years in exile, it would not have been worth it to redeem the lands of Eretz Yisrael and to establish a state here.

This dream of Jerusalem and the Temple is the spark that set Zionism afire, and whoever denies this spark will remain without Zionism and without Eretz Yisrael. How right Maya is, and how wrong your teacher is! Perhaps it is forbidden for me to speak this way about your teacher, but his error endangers the entire continuation of Zionism in general, and your kibbutz in particular.

After your matriculation exams, try to get a hold of Haim Hefer's book. It is really amazing.

Don't let those matriculation exams get to you. Believe me, the moment they're over, you won't care whether you got 80s, 90s, or 100s. Forget about the grades and take advantage of the tests to learn mainly the things that you like. I, for example, took advantage of the modern Jewish history exam to read up on Zionism, which wasn't important for the exam at all, but it was really interesting and enriching. I'm glad I didn't limit myself just to the test material, and I expanded my horizons even during the exam period. I think this approach made it possible for me to get through the exams without trauma, and even with a sense of fun.

Next week, they're moving us to Tiran Island, a small island in the Red Sea off the coast of Sharm el-Sheikh. We'll be next to Sharm, so I think we'll be able to meet. Tell me exactly where you'll be, and I will try to reach you. I'll be happy to take advantage of the opportunity and to give a lecture or hold a talk with the whole class. Maybe it can be something about Sinai in the Bible or about Israel's route in the desert during the Exodus. I think that can be interesting, with you hiking through the Sinai.

Looking forward to seeing you,

Take care,

Dov

ב"ה

3 Tammuz [July 3, 1973], Tiran

Dear Talia,

Listen, this is simply amazing. Incredible! Just a second. Let me start from the beginning. Sunday night we reached Sharm el-Sheikh from Ras Sudr. Since the boat to Tiran Island only sets out in the afternoon, we took advantage of Monday morning and we hopped over to the Ras Um Sid beach, next to Sharm, to go scuba diving. We got goggles and snorkels at the diving club in Sharm in exchange for a few liras and we were ready.

The beach is really beautiful. Clean, yellow sand, a whole lot of interesting seashells, and water as blue and tranquil as looking in the mirror. Out of the water, the water looks blue-green, and you can't even imagine what lies beneath the surface. We went into the water and we started swimming, facedown in the water. At first, near the shore, there were a lot of gray boulders with some fish swimming between them. It wasn't anything special.

After several minutes I heard a shout. I raised my head and I saw someone signaling to me to swim toward him. I did so, and when I reached him he signaled for me to put my head back in the water. Then I got the shock of my life. Beneath me was a cliff going hundreds of meters down. The whole cliff was made of coral in a rainbow of colors, such as I had never seen in my life. All the colors I could imagine were there. Between the corals swam enormous schools of fish of every variety, color, and size imaginable.

The sight was really amazing – as though you had been placed in an imaginary world of infinite colors in constant motion, joining and separating at enormous speeds. Everything was moving – the fish, the corals, the bizarre sea flora, sending out branches in all directions. I froze in place for five or ten minutes. It was so unbelievable! After several minutes I raised my head out of the water and I shouted with all my might: "How glorious Your works, O Lord!" [Psalms 104:24]. Over and over I shouted these words, which expressed everything I felt at that moment. One of my friends swam over to me and asked if I needed any help. When he understood what I was shouting, he almost wanted to hit me, because I had really scared him. For a long, long time we stayed there. We just couldn't budge. My lieutenant had to pull us away by force, and to threaten us that whoever missed the boat would end up in jail.

In short, we didn't miss the boat, and now we've been on Tiran for more than twenty-four hours. It's a small, fascinating island, with several military installations on it, which we guard. But the amazing sight of that coral reef never leaves me for even a moment. Every time I close my eyes, I see that wall of coral jutting out in all directions with the tens of thousands of colorful fish.

Now tell me, Talia, whether after an experience like that anyone could entertain the thought that there is no God that created the universe, that there is no higher power that made all these marvelous things that we've got in our world. Could they say it's all coincidence? That it happened by itself? How is it possible not to understand, not to believe? "How glorious Your works, O Lord! You made them all with wisdom. The earth is full of Your creations."

You see, Talia? I listened to your advice and I made sure not to miss scuba diving at Sharm. If I get another chance, I'll make sure to go again. Thank you.

I haven't yet received from you any letter or any note about dates and routes for your trip. The sooner I know, the better, so I can arrange my guarding schedule (and my breaks) accordingly.

Looking forward to your arrival,

Take care,

Dov

July 5, 1973

Dear Dov,

That's it! We're done! Today was our last exam, on the Bible. The matriculation exams are behind me! I'm free! There is hope! There is a future!

Out of all the exams, I studied for the Bible test the most. After two years of writing you, I wanted to prove to you that even secular people study the Bible and know it.

Maya's gone crazy. She decided that she was going to study the Torah sections of the test with Rashi. In our class, we don't even know how to read Rashi script. She tried to read it by herself (with help from one of the kibbutz members, who was a yeshiva student in his youth and still remembers a lot of things our sages said), but she pretty much gave up hope. In the end she started commuting to some rabbi's wife in Kfar Hasidim where she studied the relevant chapters with Rashi. She told everyone that she would use Rashi's comments to answer the test questions, and not the views of biblical criticism, and she didn't care at all what grade she got. It was important to her to study the Bible the way Jews learned Torah through the generations – with midrashim and with Rashi's commentary. In short, none of the threats and warnings by her Bible teacher and by her parents that she was liable to fail – since we are tested in the Bible according to science and not according to Rashi – made any dent.

In her exam, wherever she could, she wrote Rashi's interpretations based on the explanations of the rabbi's wife. During the test, she winked at me every time she mentioned Rashi, and that was really a lot of times. Now we'll see what comes of her test. She no longer cares, because she feels she belongs to another world, the world of the religious. At the start of August, after the Sinai trip, she'll be joining a Bnei Akiva settlement group. I am already starting to miss her now.

We're going to the Sinai on July 15, and we will arrive at Sharm on the eighteenth, because we'll be spending one day in

Nuweiba and one day in Dahab. Maybe you'll be able to spend Shabbat with us, July 21? That would be wonderful. You could make Kiddush for us, and maybe we'll want to hear a lecture as well. Try for it!

Take care,

Talia

AUGUST 2, 1973

Dear Dov,

Today Maya was drafted. She was running around until the last minute, because the rabbi's wife from Kfar Hasidim told her that girls shouldn't join the army.

Maya went into a panic, and she called up all the girls in her settlement group, who strongly encouraged her to enlist all the same. In the end, she called Hanan Porat, who told her that if she enlists in Nahal in the Bnei Akiva framework, then it's okay. Only after talking with Hanan did she calm down, and she went to the induction office at peace with herself. I accompanied her to the induction office (just her parents and I accompanied her). You can't imagine how much I cried before she got on the bus. I felt like this was not just a parting for several weeks. Apparently I was saying goodbye to my best friend, who was going off to another world. I hope things will always be good for her the way they are now. She has integrated wonderfully within her settlement group. Before they got on the bus, they all danced and sang Bnei Akiva songs, and she looked so much like she belonged to them. God! Fix things so that we will always stay good friends and keep in touch, even if she lives in a religious town.

How good it was that you came to visit us in Sharm! All the kids enjoyed your talk about Mount Sinai in the Bible, and until today a lot of kids are still debating about whether Mount Sinai is in the southern Sinai or the northern Sinai. You should just know that some of the kids were insulted that you didn't agree to eat with us. We prepared special food for you, which we bought in the grocery store in Sharm, because we wanted you to eat with us. I didn't exactly get what was wrong with the food we prepared for you. It hurts me so much that religious and secular Jews can't eat together. When all is said and done, we're all Jews.

I too am starting to get organized for my service in Beit She'an. Next week I've got a week of orientation, where we'll learn about life in development towns, and we'll also learn methods of providing counseling and guidance. I really can't wait! I'm getting excited as I prepare to leave the kibbutz, and I'm so interested to meet new people and new worlds. For eighteen years we lived on a kibbutz, literally in a cocoon, and now the moment has come to go out into the world and to encounter real life. Take care of yourself, Soldier, in your friendly little island.

Write a lot.

Take care,

Talia

ב"ה

12 Av 5733 [August 10, 1973], Tiran

Dear Talia,

I am writing you literally during the last minutes before Shabbat comes in. The view from the western guard post where I am presently stationed is really amazing. The sun is setting over the Sinai mountains, and the Red Sea is turning really red (making me understand the source of the name). It's so beautiful and quiet all around, as though the whole world is being decorated in preparation for Shabbat. It's as though there is no one in the world but me right now, surrounded by the crimson waters and the black mountains. Who would have believed that in such a beautiful world there could be wars and death and sorrow and suffering? Sometimes I imagine myself building a home on this small island and raising my children here. Could any place be more beautiful? What a pity there's no religious town in Sinai.

Perhaps at the end of my yeshiva/army program I'll try to organize a settlement group that will establish, in this lovely place,
a religious settlement with a serious yeshiva. Perhaps we'll call
the town Tarshish. Enough of that. I'm getting carried away
with my dreams, and Shabbat is coming soon.

Believe me, Talia, I too was very sorry that I couldn't eat
with you. The food you bought was great. I rely 100 percent
on the *kashrut* of the Chief Rabbinate, and all the cans and
containers you bought had full certification. There were two
problems, though, that you were not aware of (obviously, not
out of ill will). You cooked the meat in your own pot, and I
don't know if it's kosher or not, and you served the food on your
own dishes, and, unfortunately, there's no stamp of approval on
that either Next time I am your guest, remember this: (1) serve
the food cold (in the army as well, we very often eat food cold
right out of the can); and (2) serve it in disposable dishes, and
don't use your own. Hagi told me that he eats in the home of his
(irreligious) brother, whose wife learned these two basic rules:
(1) cold food out of closed containers; (2) presented in disposable utensils.

The happiest day of my life will be the day I can eat in
any Jew's home without worrying about *kashrut* problems. Yes,
I believe that day will come: "All your children shall be taught
by the Lord, and great shall be the harmony of your children"
[Isaiah 54:13]. When we all unite around faith and around the
Torah, there will be increased harmony between us. The haredim, as well, will then learn not to practice so many unnecessary
strictures, due to which, unfortunately, even Torah-observant
Jews don't always eat together. Mitnagdim [haredim who aren't
Hasidic] don't eat with Hasidim, and Hasidim don't eat with
Mitnagdim. There are also Hasidim who don't eat with other
Hasidim, because they belong to different streams of Hasidism
(like Chabad and Ger and Belz). That hurts me and angers me
so much. After all, the dietary laws were meant to connect Jews
and to unite the Jewish people, and in the exile it became a divi-
sive factor that bred strife.

The sun is falling toward the mountaintops, and that is a sign that Shabbat is approaching. So I'll sign off here – in the southernmost tip of the State of Israel – with a wish that you have a peaceful Shabbat.

Take care,

Dov

Dear Soldier,

Your poetic letters arouse such strong yearnings for Sinai – the vast expanses, the marvelous beaches, the amazing corals, the gigantic cliffs. Everything is so big in Sinai, so different from everything we're familiar with in our tiny little land. There's a lovely song by the Southern Command rock group called "The Song of Sinai." Whenever I hear that song on the radio, I yell at everyone to be quiet: "How immense the expanses I saw in Sinai! Never saw anything like them before..."

Believe me, there couldn't be a more appropriate place for the Torah to be given to mankind. Amidst that astonishing beauty, what human being would not open his heart? What human being wouldn't feel small and insignificant faced with the immensity of the Sinai?

Today we started our work in Beit She'an. I was sent to an elementary school, where I'm helping kids with reading difficulties advance in reading and writing. We arrived on Thursday and we got organized in our apartment. We are eight kids from all sorts of kibbutzim in Israel, and we were given a furnished apartment (kind of old and dilapidated, but I'm definitely not complaining), which we are organizing according to our own tastes. We're also cooking for ourselves, and that's really fun.

On Shabbat we ate with local families, and that was a real drag. On Friday night I ate with a Moroccan family, and the food was really spicy. Since they pushed me all the time to eat more and more, I was forced to eat even though I didn't like the food at all. That night I paid the price. I ran to the bathroom over and over, and I expelled everything I'd eaten during the past year. It was awful!

I didn't know any of the tunes from the Shabbat songs they sang at the meals, and the songs didn't speak to me. Even the words I didn't understand because of their strange accent. Besides everything else, I goofed up. When I left the bathroom, I turned the light off, and they were a bit angry at me over that. (They're religious and don't turn on lights on Shabbat.) In short, I had a really lousy time, and I think they weren't thrilled with me either.

Tell me, Dov, what's the meaning of the strange custom of not turning on lights on Shabbat? I understand that every human being deserves a day of rest once a week. That is a lovely, ethical idea (did the Jews start Shabbat, or did other nations have something similar?). But I don't understand why it's forbidden to turn on lights on Shabbat. After all, we're talking about lightly touching a switch, an act that involves no effort, and it makes Shabbat much more pleasant and fun. I am certain that this time you won't be able to come up with an interesting explanation, because this is something so strange, that for sure, even you, with all your philosophy, won't succeed in explaining it. And please don't tell me that that is what the Torah says, because you know that that's not enough for me. And besides, electricity didn't exist in the time of the Bible, so you also can't say that that's what the Torah says. In short, take advantage of your last days in Sinai to think up a good answer (and maybe this time you'll finally say that I'm right, and that you really should turn on lights on Shabbat).

Enjoy every moment in the Sinai, and if you get another chance to go scuba diving, don't miss it.

Take care of yourself, Soldier, and come home safely.

See you,

Talia

ב"ה

Dear Talia,

Indeed, these are my last days in Sinai. On Wednesday we are supposed to be discharged, and already by Sunday we'll be back in yeshiva. After half a year in the army, I miss yeshiva so much! Although even in the army I tried to learn Torah between patrols and guard duties, and even a little bit during guard duties (which wasn't quite right), it was still far from the atmosphere of yeshiva, in which hundreds of boys sit together learning. The noise in the study hall is sometimes deafening, but it so much pulls you into it and strengthens you and prods you, that even someone who doesn't enjoy learning Torah so much has to be smitten by the environment and drawn into the world of books and study. Every day I'm in yeshiva I feel like I am advancing a little, ascending spiritually a little, flourishing a little, and for me, that is a phenomenal experience.

In several more days, I'll be back in yeshiva with my fascinating teachers and Torah lectures, with our *rosh yeshiva*[1] and his enlightening talks; with our study partners and challenging questions; with our inspiring Shabbat melodies, prayers, and dancing. After such a hard, debilitating half year, how good it is to return to the world of Torah and holiness.

It is hard for me to imagine myself serving for three consecutive years in the army without the integrative *hesder* program, which enables me to return to yeshiva after every half year military stint and to recharge my batteries. This seems so right to me and so important – whoever invented this track had to be a genius. I know that right now I'm getting you angry, because you want the soldier you correspond with to serve three full, consecutive years. But what are you going to do? The spiritual needs of a religious boy are different from the needs and problems of a secular boy.

---

[1] Head of a yeshiva.

I too had years when I wondered about a lot of Shabbat prohibitions, like turning lights on, writing, playing musical instruments, and all sorts of other activities that involve no physical effort and can even make Shabbat more pleasant. I too asked myself why Jewish law insists on forbidding the use of all the electronic devices like radio and telephone. What's wrong with listening to a nice concert or talking to a friend on the telephone?

One day in yeshiva high school, I came across a little book by Rabbi Binyamin Efrati (who was our educational director there) called *She'arim el HaYahadut* [Gateways to Judaism]. It's got a wonderful article about Shabbat.

Rabbi Efrati explains the meaning of Shabbat as a "reminder of the Creation act." The Torah tells us that Shabbat is a reminder that "in six days God made the heavens and the earth, and on the seventh day He rested" [Exodus 31:17]. I always understood the connection between Shabbat and Creation superficially – when I work for six days and rest on the seventh, I remember the Creation, because God too engaged in Creation for six days, and then rested on the seventh. Rabbi Efrati offers a much deeper and more interesting explanation (I think he bases himself on Rabbi Samson Raphael Hirsch in his book *Horeb*):

Man dominates nature through science and technology – he changes nature. He creates new tools and devices. He harnesses the powers of nature for his needs and to serve him. Man's control over nature can easily turn into a feeling of arrogance, and in the course of time can even make him forget God and rebel against the Torah. Shabbat is intended to restrict man's feeling of power and domination, and to remind him that the world does not belong to him. There is a God in the world who created the universe and created man, and man cannot do whatever he feels like. Rather, he must behave in accordance with the mission that God has given him.

How can man be reminded of this? What is there to freshen man's awareness that he is "standing before God," to heighten his humility as a creation of God and an emissary of God? Judaism's main way of doing this is through Shabbat. On Shabbat (keeping Jewish law, of course), man ceases all the activities by which he expresses his control over nature, his enormous power as a creator and as a partner in creation. He brings that part of his life to expression through his six days of work and productivity, but on Shabbat he "restores the world to its owner" (I particularly remember that phrase). On this day, during which man is restricted, during which he cannot make or change or create anything, on this day he recalls his true status as a man and as a being who was created, and not, God forbid, as the sole master of the universe. This idea is so nice and simple and true that I was surprised at myself that I never thought of it before I read it in Rabbi Efrati's book.

According to this explanation, the activities forbidden by Jewish law on Shabbat are not just a matter of "work" or of physical effort, but they are activities involving dominating nature and creating differences in the status of the world. (Jewish law calls these activities *melechet mahshevet* [work involving thought], because man's thinking finds expression through such activities, by means of which he takes control over nature.)

Since reading Rabbi Efrati's words, my Shabbat has become much more profound and meaningful. Every time I want to do a forbidden action, I remind myself that the world does not belong to me, and that it is forbidden for me to do whatever I feel like. The world belongs to God, and I am just an agent who has to fulfill the task I was charged with, precisely as laid down by God in the Torah. This thought, which comes back to me on Shabbat dozens of times (every time I feel like turning on a light, or the radio, or the oven, etc.), afterwards accompanies me all week long and strengthens my connection to God and to Torah. For me, this is the meaning of Jewish law, which fashions our awareness through action, and not just through words and utterances. *Sefer HaHinuch* [The book of education] taught that "Man's heart is influenced by action," and not by preaching and sermons alone.

In the case of Shabbat, this principle can be worded a bit differently: "Man's heart is influenced by nonactivity, or by avoidance of activity." What a powerful educational tool Shabbat is, when it is observed with all its laws. How it deepens faith, strengthens humility and modesty, and increases one's power of self-control.

Obviously, Shabbat is not alone. Also the *kashrut* laws, and the laws of modesty, and the family purity laws all shape the Jew as a person capable of controlling himself and his passions. We've already spoken a great deal about this ability to restrain oneself and to delay gratification as a key to humane, moral behavior, without which man turns into a wild beast, an uncontrollable, unbearable creature. You think I wasn't hungry when I was your guest, but the law that forbids me to eat nonkosher food prevented me from satisfying my hunger and forced me to wait several hours until I returned to the camp (where there were cans of cold cuts and corn, which are a real delicacy when you're hungry).

In short, all of these halachic frameworks, on the one hand, deepen one's religious faith and humility, and on the other hand strengthen one's self-control and self-restraint. As far as I am concerned, these two educational processes are essential to shaping a moral, idealistic person, and surely we all long to be that way, or at least to advance in that direction.

Hey! I went on too long and my gear isn't set up yet. The boat's arriving in several hours, and it will bring our replacements to the island. How happy I am to be finishing up my service on this little island, but I'm parting from it with a touch of sadness as well. How many fine hours of peace and quiet I had here! How many breathtaking spots I discovered on this little island! Tiran, I'll miss you.

Take care,

Until we meet again,

Dov

SEPTEMBER 4, 1973

Dear Dov,

You'll be receiving this letter in the yeshiva you're so happy to be returning to. I am going to miss your letters from Sinai describing your experiences with scuba diving and the scenery. Once more I will have to get used to the address: Yeshivat Kerem B'Yavneh / Mobile Post Evtah, rather than Army Post 2083/Tzahal.[1]

Here in Beit She'an, we are slowly becoming accustomed to the work. In the morning, I work in the elementary school with children who have trouble reading. They are really sweet children, and they are always telling me experiences from their families (all of them have a lot of brothers and sisters), but reading and writing is the last thing on their minds.

The work I do in the evening is much harder. That's when we work with older people who barely know how to read and write. I've got three elderly women, all three of them already grandmothers, who don't know how to do anything but sign their own names. When I come to them, they are very often reciting Psalms, but they recite them from memory. They don't read them out of a book. The work with them is hard and frustrating, because not only do they lack motivation, but we don't really have a common language. I barely understand what they are saying due to their Moroccan accents. Due to this frustration, two boys have already left the group. They're signed up for the Nahal Infantry Brigade, and apparently they will be going to new settlements in the southern Jordan Valley near Jericho. That's not far from Beit She'an, so we'll be able to keep on meeting. We've now got four girls and two boys in our apartment, a clear majority for the girls, so we decide what we listen to on the radio.

It's amazing to see the big differences between the generations in this town. The elderly are almost all religious. They

---

[1] Tzahal is the acronym for the Hebrew name of the Israel Defense Forces, Tzva L'Hagana L'Yisrael.

go twice a day to synagogue, and they spend a lot of time there. The second generation, which grew up in Israel, are almost all secular, although most of them come to synagogue on Shabbat. The children of that second generation almost all learn in the town's secular school (the religious school is small and quite run down), and on Shabbat they go to meetings of HaNoar Ha'Oved[2] and to the soccer stadium. (We run the Working Youth branch, mostly on Shabbat, but also a little bit during the week).

Another thing. The religious people here are different from you. They don't philosophize the way you do, and they don't study out of large Talmudic tomes like you do. All day long they pray and recite Psalms and read a book called *Hok L'Yisrael*. One time I asked one of the people we work with to explain what this *Hok L'Yisrael* is, and he barely succeeded in telling me something I could understand. Maybe you'll be able to give me a better explanation. I don't understand how they don't go nuts from all their praying and reciting Psalms. After all, they repeat the same prayers every single day. Doesn't that bore them? It's like chewing your cud. The same thing over and over (I hope you're not insulted by my comparison, but that's what occurs to me every time I see those old men praying). I'm not surprised that the young people don't want to come to synagogue, because it really does look boring to me – even aggravating.

Shabbats here as well are downright boring. Either they're praying in the synagogue or they're eating. Most of the families eat on their porches, because it's so darn hot in the houses. In general, the whole clan eats together, because you've got a lot of people here who have relatives in town. The only place in town that's interesting on Shabbat is the sports stadium. In the afternoon, when it gets a bit less hot, everyone goes there and watches the weekly game involving the HaPoel team of Beit She'an. That's a third-string minor league team, but everyone's really proud of it. Once or twice a year the team wins, but usually it loses. That doesn't stop anyone from going really crazy over the team.

---

[2] HaNoar Ha'Oved is the name of an Israeli youth movement founded in 1924.

In short, life here is quite boring, and what keeps me going is our apartment experience. We have fun together. We cook all kinds of crazy dishes for ourselves and stay awake half the night, and we gab about all the topics in the world. It's really a feeling of being adults.

We're missing someone like you to philosophize a bit and to quote from the Bible, but instead of the Bible we've got a girl who really knows all the books by Ayn Rand[3] by heart, and quotes from her all the time. Because of Ayn Rand, she has decided to leave the kibbutz and to live in the city, because the kibbutz interferes with the individual's independence. We're always trying to convince her that the kibbutz provides the proper balance between individualism and collectivism, and that human beings are social creatures who need to forgo some part of their independence in order to be part of the community. But she hardly listens to us, because Ayn Rand's books have already brainwashed her. She's constantly talking about "self-actualization" and "personal fulfillment," and that everyone has to worry only about himself and not to deal with others at all. This philosophy really gets me mad, but I have a pretty hard time proving to her that she is wrong. I look forward to your help.

I hope that in yeshiva, as well, you'll keep on writing a lot. I really wait with great yearning for your letters.

Take care,

Talia

❖ ❖ ❖

ב"ה

17 ELUL 5733 [SEPTEMBER 13, 1973]

Dear Talia,

Finally, we're back in yeshiva, which we missed so badly. We really pounced on the Talmud volumes and the other books, as

---

[3] An American author who became famous during the sixties and seventies, chiefly thanks to her books *Atlas Shrugged* and *The Fountainhead*, which preached extreme individualism.

well as the lectures and talks. It's the feeling of a person who has walked through the desert for several months and has finally reached an oasis with water and shade and sweet dates. It's just like that. The lectures are so sweet! Once more our brains are working and our thoughts are soaring in the heavens; our eyes are searching the fine print for answers to questions, and not for suspicious characters in the dark night.

It looks to me like you don't think much of the people you work with. From your letter, I get the impression that you view them as a bit primitive and old-fashioned. I'd like to add a bit of perspective. It's thanks to primitive people like these that the Jewish people survived for thousands of years. Yes, you heard me right (better yet – you *read* me right). These people and others like them, simple and innocent, but strong and unswerving in their faith, held out for thousands of years against countless forms of pressure and coercion, against pogroms and expulsions, against an ocean of hatred and anti-Semitism. Yes, with their boring prayers and their chapters of Psalms that they repeat and their *Hok L'Yisrael*, which they barely understand, they remained faithful to their God, their Jewishness, their people, their homeland, their identity. For thousands of years, the nations tried to break this little nation, and it's thanks to people like these that we still exist. It's thanks to people like these that we returned to Eretz Yisrael and to Jerusalem. It's thanks to people like these that we still continue to study the Bible and the Midrash, the Mishna and the Talmud, the Rambam and Rabbi Yehuda HaLevi.

By the way, *Hok L'Yisrael* is the name of a book on the weekly Torah portion. Every day one reads from it not just a fraction of the weekly portion, but also chapters of Mishna and Talmud, Midrash and the Zohar, which is the basic work of Kabbala.

Yes, those boring prayers are part of the secret – the secret of Israel's survival. It's very boring, three or five times a day, to repeat the prayer "Build Jerusalem, the holy city, speedily in our day." Yet thanks to that persistence and stubbornness, and thanks to that endless repetition, we have succeeded in doing the unbelievable: educating generations of Jews, who over the course of thousands of years did not forget their ancient homeland and were privileged to return to it after such a long exile.

Can you make light of such people? Do you have the right to make light of those prayers? You, especially, must treat them with dignity, since we have not yet seen that the kibbutz and the Jewish state have succeeded in producing something better. Look at how many boys from your kibbutz not only don't want to continue living on the kibbutz, but not even in Eretz Yisrael. Look at how many of the boys on your kibbutz are willing to marry volunteers even if those volunteers haven't undergone conversion. Maybe it's due to the ease and speed with which you all gave up on the prayer book and on the boring prayers and on the study of *Hok L'Yisrael*, which you don't understand so well. Israeli education shows no signs that it will succeed in passing on Judaism for another two thousand years. I am in doubt whether in even another twenty years it will hold fast as an education that raises proud Jews and loyal Zionists. Let's salute those simple, "primitive" Jews, who, in my eyes, possess giant souls and noble spirits found in no other nation.

Also, as far as your rejecting that "boring" Shabbat, I'm not sure that will prove justified in the long run. It's really "boring" to sit at a Shabbat meal for hours without a radio, television, telephone, or record player. But think about how much the family gains, studying together and chatting together and strengthening the bonds between parents and children, and between the children, who sometimes see each other very little during the week. What wisdom (divine, obviously, and not human) there is to Jewish law, which insisted on leaving at least one day of the week without any of the innovations or temptations of technology, without any running around with modern forms of transportation. There's one day when you stay home with the whole family, and the telephone doesn't bother you and the radio doesn't distract you. Everything is devoted to the family. Everything is inner driven, not outer driven. Those

Shabbat meals that you poked mild fun at, yes, those Shabbat meals that you are seeing in Beit She'an on the porch with the whole clan – it's thanks to them that the Jewish family was a source of power and strength and inspiration. It's thanks to them that the Jewish family stood fast and remained strong and stable even in the stormiest periods of Jewish history.

Has Israeli culture created an alternative to Shabbat meals, to holiday ceremonies, to Jewish tradition? I hear from you that even the ceremonies that the kibbutz has fashioned, like the first-fruits ceremony you told me about, already don't attract the youth. So who are we to make fun of traditions and customs that have held fast for so many years and preserved the identity of the Jewish people and the stability of the Jewish family?

I just turned on the radio for a moment to hear the news, and I'm jumping for joy. Our air force downed thirteen Syrian MiGs in a large air battle that took place over the Syrian skies. What a great army we've got! What a marvelous air force! How is it possible not to be proud of our pilots!

On second thought, I'm wondering what reaction we can expect from the Syrians. They certainly won't remain silent at such a humiliation and will try to retaliate. Who knows if a war won't break out from the violent exchange that will occur following such a heady victory? The Six-Day War also grew out of an exchange of attacks between us and the Syrians on the background of a Syrian diversion.

You know, throughout the month before Rosh Hashana, it's customary to add a psalm at the end of every morning and evening prayer: "Of David. The Lord is my light and my help; whom should I fear?" [Psalms 27:1]. It's forbidden for us to be afraid of anything other than God. After all, He has been accompanying the Jewish people for almost four thousand years, and the fact is that we are still around. All the great powers that harmed us have disappeared from the earth, and only we have survived and returned to our land and downed thirteen (!!) MiGs. Only from such a perspective can we understand what it says later in the same chapter: "Should an army besiege me, my heart would have no fear. Should war beset me, I would place my trust in this" (verse 3).

My father likes to make use of *gematriyot* (the numerical values of the Hebrew letters). One time he showed me something very interesting that answers a not-so-simple question about these verses. What is the meaning of "in this" [Hebrew *b'zot*] in the above verse? In what is King David placing his trust? The answer my father gave me is based on a liturgical poem customarily recited on Rosh Hashana and Yom Kippur, "U'Netane Tokef." That poem concludes with the proclamation "Repentance, prayer, and charity ward off the evil decree." In most of the High Holiday prayer books there is a small addition: Above the word "prayer" appears the Hebrew word *kol* [outcry], above the word "repentance" appears the Hebrew word *tzom* [fasting], and above the word "charity" appears the Hebrew word *mamon* [money]. Each of these three Hebrew words has the numerical value of 136. (For example, the word *kol*, is composed of the letter *kuf*, with a numerical value of 100; the letter *vav*, with a value of six; and the letter *lamed*, with a value of thirty.) The three words together amount to 408, which is precisely the numerical value of *zot*, "this," from the expression *bezot* above. In other words, King David is saying that he places his trust in prayer, repentance, and charity. Isn't that nice? (Whoever is unaccustomed to using *gematriyot* may be unimpressed by such novelties. My father is really enthusiastic about this approach, and he devotes a lot of time to it.)

I interpret the verse according to its plain meaning: "in this" – I place my faith in our belief. Only faith in the God of Israel can give us the strength to continue withstanding the great challenges and the difficult trials that still await us. Without faith, I am convinced that, God forbid, we will disintegrate and be badly weakened, but with faith we shall advance from one success to another. "Should an army besiege me, my heart would have no fear. Should war beset me, I would place my trust in *this*."

Talia, Rosh Hashana is approaching, and I want to wish you a good, blessed year. I especially wish that you should learn to like the people that you work with this year. They are so different from yourself, but you can still learn so much from them. If you open up to them, you will discover that these simple people possess enormous spiritual and cultural wealth, wealth which is not just an accumulation of their life experiences but of...four thousand years of Jewish history (you must for sure have guessed).

So once more, have a good year,

And take care,

Dov

Dear Dov,

You frightened me a bit with your talk about war, so please don't do that again. I pray that there won't be any war, and that we will all have a quiet, tranquil year. I add my own blessings to yours for the coming year. You are right, that I need to be more open to new things I wasn't familiar with before, and to people who at first glance seem downright bizarre to me. I hope I will be able to muster the inner resources needed for such openness, and I hope I will really gain a lot culturally. I spent eighteen years on my kibbutz, literally in a cocoon, and there was almost no variety – everyone spoke with the same style and everyone looked more or less the same. In Beit She'an, everything is so different. I owe myself the openness that you speak of, the ability not to put on airs before these people, but to learn from them. In short, you're right. Recently I find myself saying again and again, "Dov is right." I find myself asking again and again, "What would Dov say about this?" I find myself trying to look at all sorts of things not from the perspective of an eighteen-year-old kibbutz girl, but from the perspective of a girl belonging to a four-thousand-year-old nation. And I find myself wondering again and again, "Talia, what's with you? Are you starting to become religious? Talia! Are you too being bitten by the Maya bug?"

By the way, I met with Maya on the kibbutz last Shabbat. I told her about the thoughts and questions that have been haunting me recently, and she was enormously pleased. She's all set to get me a place in her settlement group. She nudges

With his tank unit, at Julis training base, under the command of Avigdor Kahalani

me, saying, "What's wrong with your being a kibbutznik, but on a religious kibbutz? We'll continue there with all the values we were raised on, but we'll become attached to the Torah and to Jewish tradition. That will give our values a lot more strength." She then repeats, "We won't be giving up a thing. We'll just be expanding our horizons and making them more profound." And I am afraid that I'm starting to break down, that I am starting to be convinced. "At least try," a little voice inside me whispers every time I receive a letter from you and every time I meet with Maya.

Yet then I get panicky and I say to myself: "Shall I too start quarreling with my parents about *kashrut* in their home and about setting Shabbat clocks? Shall I too, like Maya, cut myself off from all the other kids I grew up with, who I'm so attached to?" And then I decide: "No. Out of the question." And always when these thoughts crop up, I go to sleep and forget it all, because it's quite frightening to think about Maya's path. How I admire her for her courage, her stubbornness, her determination.

I know (I heard this from you when we met in Sharm el-Sheikh) that you too wonder about what path you should take – not like me, but about where to continue your studies – about continuing on in yeshiva or going to university. It would really suit you to learn philosophy in university. I'd grant you a PhD in philosophy this minute if I could. My wish for you is that whatever decision you make this year will be the best decision for you, and that you should be at peace with the decision, and happy with its results.

Have a good, sweet year,

Take care,

Talia

ב"ה

4 Tishrei 5734 [September 30, 1973]

Dear Talia,

I turned on the radio several minutes ago after three days of not hearing the news (two days of Rosh Hashana and the Shabbat that follows). They started the report with an announcement about Arab terrorists kidnapping Jews in Austria who were in the process of making aliya from Russia. The Austrians, obviously, surrendered immediately to the terrorists and announced that they were stopping Jewish emigration from Russia to Israel via Austria. Suddenly, the rumor we had been hearing became an official announcement: It's true! In recent years, tens of thousands of Jews have been streaming from Russia to Israel. None of the Russians' strategies for keeping the Jews in Russia did them any good – not their Iron Curtain and not their iron fist and not the beckoning doors of their prisons.

The Jews are a stubborn people, and their God is even more stubborn. He promised to return the Jewish people from the four corners of the earth to Eretz Yisrael when the time of redemption arrived, and now, after two thousand years, He is keeping His promise: "Even if your outcasts are at the ends of the world, from there the Lord your God will gather you, from there He will fetch you. And the Lord your God will bring you to the land that your fathers possessed, and you shall possess it; and He will make you more prosperous and more numerous than your fathers" (Deuteronomy 30:4–5).

It's no coincidence that the Arabs are trying every which way to stop the waves of aliya to Israel. It's no coincidence that during the Mandate, the British tried every way possible to stop the waves of aliya to Israel. They're not afraid of the military might of several more million Jews. They're chiefly afraid of the religious significance of the Jewish people gathering together into their land. Both Christianity and Islam will fall, because God is fulfilling His promise and His covenant for the Jewish people, even though both Islam and Christianity view the Jews as a people that God abandoned.

Now it is becoming clear that neither Christianity nor Islam is the continuation of the Jewish people. Rather, the Jewish people were, and remain, the chosen people, whom God is redeeming in such a miraculous and supernatural fashion after two thousand years of exile. How that possibility frightens them! So they make enormous efforts to halt the process of Israel's redemption. Yet with the help of the God of Israel, they will not succeed. Their plot will be foiled, and the Jewish people will continue coming to Israel. They will continue settling throughout our Holy Land, from the Sinai to the Golan. They will continue studying and teaching Torah. Nothing anyone does against us, inside or outside Israel, will help them one bit. The redemption will continue on and on, and will grow and expand.

And amidst this whole great process, I continue to ask myself: How shall I contribute to the redemption process? Perhaps as a scientist, who contributes to our country's scientific and technological advancement, thus helping to consolidate Israel's economy so that no one can threaten us and place economic pressure on us. Or perhaps as a physician, who performs kind deeds for people in difficult circumstances, and succeeds in adding to their happiness, health, and vigor, and to their ability to smile. In general I enjoy studying the natural sciences. Even here in yeshiva I read scientific literature (chiefly brochures from the Weizmann Institute), and I believe that I will be able to succeed both in medical studies and in the natural sciences.

Yet apparently this is not my true calling. Education – that's the word that resonates for me wherever I go; that is the key to the future of the Jewish people as a people of faith, Torah, and eternal values. I pray I will be privileged to fulfill this great calling and to participate in creating one more link in the chain of the generations of the Jewish people; a link that will include the renewal of the Torah of Eretz Yisrael, the renewal of a people redeemed from a long exile, but a people that will remain attached to all the links that came before, and that will not cut itself off from them, God forbid. I believe that this is possible. I believe that, with God's help, this will occur, and I should only be so fortunate as to participate in the fulfillment of this great vision.

It's customary to wish people a good year until Yom Kippur (and according to Hasidic custom, until Hoshana Rabba, the last day of Sukkot). So once again, Talia, I wish you a good year, a year in which you will actualize all the wonderful facets of your personality. And don't be alarmed by thoughts about becoming religious. Look how happy Hagi is that he has succeeded in combining Zionism (military service that included a commander's course), academics (he is presently attending university), and the Torah he learned in yeshiva. Look how happy Maya is that she has succeeded in combining fulfillment in pioneering through the Nahal program and in kibbutz with a way life built around Torah and observance. Being religious does not mean throwing out the marvelous things that are part of your world, part of the environment that you grew up in, and part of your unique personality. When all of these fine elements are joined together to God, they only become stronger and fuller, and they endure for generations. I will always be happy to be at your side and to accompany you with advice and guidance to the best of my ability, as I have tried to do (perhaps not enough) during the last two years.

I would like to send New Year's wishes to your father as well, of whom I have good memories from serving together in the army. We had some wonderful talks, and I would like very much to keep up the contact. Please send him my warmest regards.

Be strong and brave!

All my blessings,

Take care,

Dov

OCTOBER 5, 1973 (THE DAY BEFORE YOM KIPPUR)

Dear Dov,

Today I received your letter and I am hurrying to write you back already today. I'm partly doing this because since your last letter, in which you wrote that there may be a war with Syria, I've been really worried and troubled. Something inside me is very uneasy. Today, several soldiers didn't come home for their Shabbat leave, and there are rumors about an army alert. That's just made me worry all the more. My worries have led me to a decision: This year I'm fasting on Yom Kippur and I'm going to the synagogue near our apartment. I already know several women there, and I definitely feel less of an outsider there. I'll pray for there not to be a war, for all the soldiers to be busy only with practice drills and guard duty, and not with real battles.

Well then, what do you have to say about me? Two years ago, when we started to write, would you have believed that the cynical kibbutz girl who bothers you with aggravating questions would attend synagogue and fast on Yom Kippur? (I hope I don't break down and that I succeed in completing the fast.)

How I have changed during these two years! How my world has opened up to things I never imagined even in my wildest dreams! And it's all thanks to you, Dov, thanks to your enchanting letters, thanks to my fascinating talks with you. Sometimes I think I live from letter to letter. So please, write more! I wait with such yearning for your letters!

Wishing you a marvelous year,

From me, who thinks about you a great deal,

Talia

Dov never answered this letter. Talia's fears unfortunately proved true. One day after her last letter, on Yom Kippur, October 6, 1973, the Yom Kippur War broke out. Dov was in Yeshivat Kerem B'Yavneh, and immediately after the end of the fast, he returned to his home in Jerusalem. That same night, he was drafted with the rest of his friends, students of the *hesder* yeshivot, who were among the first drafted in the war. They were transported to the Pilon military camp in the Galilee, took up positions on their tanks in an accelerated process, and already on Sunday morning raced up as the first reserve units to the Golan Heights.

During the first day of battle, Israel's positions on the Golan Heights had been breached, and large Syrian forces had swept over the Israeli positions, conquering most of the Golan Heights. In the Nafah region, the first tanks of the 679th Brigade, in which Dov served, ran up against large armored Syrian forces. Harsh battles ensued, following which the Syrian armor was halted. Dov was killed on the second day of battle (October 7) in the area of the quarry at the foot of Mount Shifon. Together with Dov, hundreds of soldiers fell in the holding action on the Golan Heights. Through their bravery and self-sacrifice, Dov and his friends helped save the Golan Heights, the ancient tribal portion of Menashe, for the Jewish people.

Following her military service, Talia returned to her kibbutz in northern Israel, where she is a member to this day. Maya participated with her friends in establishing a new religious settlement on the Golan Heights, where she is still a member. Hagi took part in establishing the town of Beit El in Samaria, where he continues to live. He teaches Bible and Jewish philosophy in several teachers' seminaries in Jerusalem.

Chapters in
Dov's Life

Dov was born in Romania on June 7, 1951, the firstborn of his parents, Avraham and Miriam. Already as a child, he stood out for his cleverness and his quick understanding. Before he had started elementary school, he could read Hungarian fluently, without his parents knowing how, or from whom, he had learned this. Dov spent only three months in school before he moved to Israel, yet he still acquired a strong command of Hungarian, which enabled him to write letters to his mother in Hungarian until his last days.

At age seven, he moved to Israel with his parents and his brother Moshe (who was three years younger). The family settled in Jerusalem, and Dov was sent to study in the Chabad elementary school in the Ir Ganim neighborhood. Although he lacked the Israeli background of his peers, he quickly stood out as an outstanding student and the teachers' favorite pupil. At the end of third grade, it was decided to move him up to fifth grade. When that did not suffice, the school recommended that his parents move him to a school on a higher level. Dov was moved to the Shilo *talmud Torah* [a Torah-intensive elementary school], where he completed fifth grade. Despite the short time he spent there, Dov managed to earn a certificate of excellence. At that time, a *talmud Torah* opened in the Bayit Vegan neighborhood, and Dov's parents decided to move him there due to its proximity to their home. Here, as well, his homeroom teacher, Rabbi Yaakov Vonderwalde, took a great liking to him, and the ties between the two continued for years.

When he completed eighth grade in the *talmud Torah*, the staff tried to influence him to continue in a *yeshiva ketana* [a Torah-intensive high school lacking secular studies]. However, with his parents' support and encouragement, Dov decided to go to the Netiv Meir yeshiva high school, where secular subjects were taught alongside Torah studies. With this decision, one already notes one of the central characteristics of Dov's personality, which became more and more marked as time went on – Dov's longing to develop his intellectual faculties and to expand his horizons. Even at Netiv Meir, where there was a concentration of above-average students from all over the country, Dov continued to stand out, and already in his first year he received a prize for excellence. His thirst for knowledge was not satisfied by his formal studies, and he read numerous books of all types – from science to fine literature – during his free time. He didn't just strive to learn from books, but from "animate books" as well – from people. The debates and discussions that went on between his roommates often continued into the wee hours of the night, with Dov driving the conversations on and on.

All the same, he didn't neglect other aspects of his personality. Despite his having come to the yeshiva high school from a *talmud Torah,* he quickly integrated among the students and took an active part in their frequent nighttime jogs, in long hikes with friends during vacations times, and in other social activities. He also strove to reach out to other students who were on the social fringes and to draw them in, an activity which figured very prominently later on at Yeshivat Kerem B'Yavneh.

When he completed high school, he was uncertain about whether to continue in full-time yeshiva or in a *hesder* track, combining Torah study with military service. Ultimately he chose *hesder.* Although he viewed Torah learning as the most important thing, he was unwilling to give up military service, which he viewed as a national duty of the highest order. In the background, there was always the possibility of academic studies at a later stage, and, toward the end of *hesder,* Dov thought a great deal about this option. Although he wanted to continue learning Torah, he was not certain that his future lay in the realm of teaching. For that reason, he thought about the possibility of pursuing university studies to attain a profession, while he would continue studying Torah for his own spiritual enhancement. On the way to battle, he told a friend who had enlisted with him that his mind was more and more set on continuing in yeshiva after he finished *hesder*.

After his initial half year of learning in Kerem B'Yavneh, in the summer of 1970, Dov went off to basic training, after which he continued in the armored corps track, including the professional tank course, followed by the TPC (Tank-Platoon-Company) exercises applying what was learned in the course, and subsequent service in the field.

Going off to the army reveals a person's character, enabling one to see who he is, not only at his Talmudic lectern, within the cocoon of the yeshiva, but how he performs in difficult and pressure-filled situations. Here is the true measure of the individual. In this test, Dov revealed an enormously strong will. Despite his not being particularly physically fit, he never broke, and he even helped others greatly in difficult moments. He particularly demonstrated his strong will in his scrupulous observance of the Torah's commandments under all circumstances. He was not tempted to take the lenient path, even regarding the minutest details. His performance as a soldier was average, perhaps due to his tendency toward dreaminess and absentmindedness, but every task and every mission he was charged with he fulfilled with great devotion, out of a deep recognition that he was thereby fulfilling a Torah commandment.

In the realm of Torah study, Dov continued to advance and became skillful at analyzing Talmudic texts and resolving questions. He especially loved in-depth study. He would attack a particular point, sometimes even a small side issue, and clarify it as much as possible, examining every available source, including rabbinic responsa not commonly referred to. He was never satisfied with superficial or partial study, always aiming to cover all aspects of a topic.

He continued to expand his intellect in secular fields as well. He regularly took out books from the National Library, read encyclopedias and journals, and even worked on solving the mathematical challenges published regularly by the Haifa Technion. His thirst for knowledge knew no bounds, and during his vacation periods he would often read in his room until two or three in the morning, turning off the lights only when his parents admonished him. He generally did not want to take money from his parents, and spent the little amounts that they persuaded him to take for purchasing books.

Due to his yearning for perfection, he often wasn't happy with himself, and for that reason he sometimes suffered from serious internal crises. He generally didn't let them ruin his learning routine, and, on the outside, one almost couldn't tell what was happening to him. He told only a few others about his inner turmoil, among them Rabbi Chaim Lipschitz, who was the *mashgiah* [the yeshiva's spiritual guidance counselor] at that time, and with whom Dov became particularly attached.

Together with his scholarly excellence, Dov was extraordinarily ethical. He sat humbly in his corner, studying his texts, and didn't try to stand out. He also developed bonds with boys who were on the social fringes, and tried to help and encourage them. He assisted his parents a lot, and during vacations he would run around taking care of various errands that his parents had a hard time doing because they were not adept at Hebrew. He approached every task seriously, without the least trace of cynicism. In his last years, he particularly adopted the practice of avoiding forbidden speech, and he devoted himself enthusiastically to studying the many laws associated with this topic, making a constant effort not to fall prey to this common, widespread sin. Also regarding other commonly overlooked sins, like falsehood and acts verging on theft, he was very careful, down to the tiniest detail.

On October 6, 1973, when Yom Kippur had ended and it became known that war had broken out, Dov was at his yeshiva, Kerem B'Yavneh. He rushed home to collect his things, and that same night he was on his way to his unit. He spent his last bus trip up to the Golan Heights reciting Psalms. His tank was hit at West Junction on the second day of the war...

Friends Talk
about Dov

From a conversation that took place in the home of Dov's parents, on the second anniversary of his passing. Participants: Simha Ansbacher, Hagi Ben-Artzi, Yitzchak Halperin, Yitzchak Heller, Moshe Lipschitz, Haim Sabato, and Reuven Klein.

Hagi: It's been two years since Dov's passing, and I think it's a good thing that such a talk is being held two years down the road. These two years have removed us a bit from the great turmoil, the great weeping, and consequently also from the tendency to exaggerate. At the same time, those two years have allowed us to see Dov more fully, to see his essence beyond – or more precisely, by way of – the many details and the minor acts.

What was really the thing that characterized Dov? What made him unique?

It seems to me that what made him special was the rare combination of a stellar personality both intellectually and ethically. We often encounter people for whom one side, the scholastic or the ethical, is dominant, while the other is neglected and tainted. What was interesting and captivating about Dov was the combination of these two, with each of them, per se, having enormous force.

Yitzchak Heller: I would like to take up the point Hagi started with. A talented person is often tainted with arrogance, with a feeling of self-importance. With Dov, that didn't happen. His excellence in the scholastic realm didn't stop him from being a simple person, from being humble. He clearly didn't consider himself important. He didn't make a big deal out of himself. This found expression in the fact that he was always ready and open to learn from everyone. Whoever spoke to him got the feeling that Dov was relating seriously to what he was hearing. This was expressed in the fact that he was ready to, as they say, "mix with the simple people," to find a common language with people who are not intellectuals, to understand them, to help them.

I was in several frameworks together with Dov – yeshiva high school, post–high school yeshiva, the army – and I noticed that wherever he was, he connected with people on the fringes, people whom society didn't understand. He came down to their level and tried to understand them and to help them, without giving them the feeling that he was doing that. And he did it all

with such simplicity, humility, and innocence. For example, he reached out to a boy who had been caught stealing, and helped him to integrate anew in society. At Kerem B'Yavneh, he had a special affinity for the students from abroad. Among the many things that we can learn from Dov, that was one of the most important.

During his studies at Yeshivat Kerem B'Yavneh. Photo taken at home on Zichron Yaakov Street, Jerusalem.

Simha: If we're talking about integration, I want to mention another type of integration that I found in Dov – between understanding and faith. Several days ago, the General Assembly of the United Nations passed a resolution condemning Zionism. I can just picture Dov hearing that decision – in one moment he could profoundly analyze the possible repercussions of such a decision, and the next moment he could forget everything, be taken up with simple faith, and, out of his enormous joy and trust in God, encouragingly slap everyone in the room on the back. It was a sort of combination of broad-minded worldliness with deep and pure faith. Dov was well versed in what was happening; he knew how to analyze situations and events in a thorough manner. Yet he also always emphasized the aspect of faith, the hand of God in every development, and he even tried to find scriptural allusions to what was happening in the present.

Yitzchak Halperin: What I see as basic to Dov's character is the trait of friendship in which he so excelled. I was privileged to be a friend of his for quite a number of years. Dov had all the characteristics of a good friend. He was always ready to make an effort to help out a friend, even if it involved a burden and a sacrifice for him. He was capable of giving a friend his class notes before a test, making it hard for him to study. You barely had to ask him. I remember that when I was in the army, he wanted to know which Shabbat I was coming home for, and then he would walk to my house on foot from Kiryat HaYovel.[1] When things were hard for me, he would do his utmost to offer me encouragement.

Hagi: I want to back up what Yitzchak said. Although Dov was a year younger than me, he was one of the only friends I could fully open my heart to about my personal problems. I felt like I was able to, and I wanted to, pour out my heart to him. The way he listened to personal things about me, he gave me the feeling that it interested him, that he cared, that he sincerely wanted to help, to give good advice. I felt like he empathized totally with what was happening to me. That was a marvelous feeling. I've got to say that until this day when I look for somebody to share with me what is bothering me, I always recall Dov.

---

[1] Kiryat HaYovel, a neighborhood in Jerusalem, is located at a distance of about three miles from the neighborhood of Bayit Vegan, where Yitzchak lived.

Haim: I'm not able to analyze Dov the way you analyze a literary figure and define what characterized him. That would be like analyzing somebody who was sitting among us. And for me, it's as though Dov is sitting among us at this moment. We were very close – from *talmud Torah,* straight through Netiv Meir, where we lived in the same room for a long time, until our shared military service. All the same, I shall attempt to point out several aspects that stand out.

One of the things that were special about Dov was his intense worldliness. He wanted to embrace the whole universe, both in thought and deed. He took an interest in everything, both in the spheres of Judaism and in the secular realm. We were together at Ras Sudr in the operational part of our service. There, in some little room, he arranged a library for himself. Whoever saw that makeshift library would have been shocked, and one time he even laughed at himself. a psychology book, an archaeology book, a book by Agnon,[2] a book about Eretz Yisrael, one of the Technion's brochures of mathematical challenges, alongside a Bible and Tractate Ketubot. It sounds like an exaggeration, but that's exactly how it was. He regularly took out books from the National Library.

Hagi: It was my bitter duty, after Dov fell, to return to the National Library a pile of books that were left in his possession. I recall that the list included a book by Judge Bazak[3] about parapsychological phenomena in Judaism, as well as a book about the Israeli economy...demonstrating enormous breadth.

Haim: He read through the entries of the *Hebrew Encyclopedia,* solved mathematical challenges published regularly by the Haifa Technion. His mother once said that sometimes she

---

[2] Shai Agnon (1888–1970) was a Nobel Prize laureate in literature and one of the central figures in modern Hebrew fiction.

[3] Yaakov Bazak (b. 1925) was the vice president of the district court in Jerusalem until 1995 and the longest-serving justice in the State of Israel's history.

would find him before dawn lying in bed and reading, and she would have to yell at him so he would go to sleep. In the realm of Torah, as well, he didn't limit himself to Talmud, but also studied Jewish philosophy, moral tracts, and the literature of Jewish law. At one point he was very interested in Hasidism (an article by Dov about the first Lubavitcher Rebbe was published in Kerem B'Yavneh's journal).

Moshe: My relationship with Dov was not in the realm of Torah, nor in the realm of fine character. I loved to talk with him about scientific innovations – in chemistry and physics. The interest he took in scientific problems surprised me, and it didn't jibe so well for me with his image as a yeshiva student. Because our connection was in science, Dov told me about his uncertainty about whether to continue on in yeshiva or to go to university. I know that at one point he longed to study medicine.

Reuven: Following what Haim and Moshe said, I think it's worth emphasizing that even though Dov had such a multifaceted personality, he was, above all else, a yeshiva student. Haim Nehorai told me that Dov told him, a few days before the war, that it was clear to him that he was going to remain in yeshiva. This fact is not just interesting per se. I think it also has symbolic meaning. After all the uncertainties that were formed on the background of Dov's varied interests, he remained a yeshiva student, and his affinity for Torah was the main thing for him.

Haim: I would like to relate to what Yitzchak (Halperin) said about Dov's quality of friendship. That's a very interesting point. On the one hand, Dov was a sociable type who never set himself apart from the crowd. I remember that at Netiv Meir he would do all sorts of slightly crazy things, like running at night to Ein Kerem, just to show that he was one of the guys. At the same time, he also excelled at serving God as an individual. He loved to be alone, to be with himself. On class trips he would sometimes disappear and we would have to look for him. It generally turned out that he had simply gotten waylaid by something that interested him. That was something very out of the ordinary, considering the communal-oriented education we received in our yeshivot, an education that focused on the nation, on society, on the settlement group, on the class unit, etc.

Another way that Dov was special was in his strong connection to family. We all have that, but not to such a great degree. I remember well the first year that Moshe, Dov's brother, was at Netiv Meir. Dov spent many nights with me and with other friends thinking about what to do so that Moshe would become acclimated to the yeshiva.

Yitzchak Heller: When the war broke out, and we set out at the end of Yom Kippur from Kerem B'Yavneh to Jerusalem, the whole way he thought about Moshe, who was then in the army. At Ramle, a bus full of armored division soldiers drove by, and he tried to check if somebody there knew his brother and knew where he was and how he was doing.

Haim: I was also surprised by the sensitivity he displayed over what his parents were doing for him. I don't know if they knew how strongly he felt this. Everything he did – buying books, giving charity, etc. – he did with the feeling that the money wasn't his. In an argument he had once, he told me, "I know my parents work hard so I will have it good, and I have to show consideration for what they ask of me." He had a very high, very rare level of gratitude.

Yitzchak Heller: In that regard, it's important to mention that Dov made a very big contribution to his parents' integration in Israel. His parents worked, and they also didn't have a good grasp of Hebrew, and the brunt of running household errands fell on him. During his vacations he would spend a lot of time running around between offices. He expressed his gratitude to his parents, among other ways, through regular letter writing (he made an effort to write his mother in Hungarian), and through sending gifts on birthdays.

Simha: Haim spoke of Dov's worldliness and his broad horizons. I would specifically like to stress how thorough he was. Whatever topic he learned, he strove to clarify every problem as much as possible, to examine every source that could make the picture clearer. He was never too lazy to look up all the recommended sources, even when the matter was clear without further examination. This longing to examine every topic fully would sometimes aggravate his study partners. The study partner would suggest moving on and leaving the difficulties as matters to be dealt with later, but Dov would insist: "I've got to understand this point all the way." If he didn't understand something, artillery bombs could be whistling overhead and he wouldn't hear them. When he was unsatisfied with the resolution of a particular topic, he would remain in the study hall until he understood it and had solved the problem, even if he arrived last in the dining hall.

Hagi: His longing for perfection found expression not only through Torah learning, but through deeds as well, through fulfillment. At some point in yeshiva we decided –Dov and I – to study the laws of avoiding forbidden speech. We devoted a lot of time and effort to this, and we worked on it quite thoroughly. What surprised me afterwards was how Dov applied the laws we had learned down to the last detail. When we were talking, he would sometimes cut me off to remind me of some law that we had learned that I was liable to violate through one mode of expression or another. He would weigh his words in a very serious and precise manner.

I remember I was impressed by how he put the theories in practice, by the seriousness and the perfection with which he strove to apply every law we had learned. The laws of guarding one's tongue are complex indeed, with a lot of allowances and prohibitions that must be weighed subtly. He also published a long essay on this topic in one of the editions of *B'Lechtecha BaDerech* (the journal published by Kerem B'Yavneh). Almost always when I think about Dov, it's accompanied by thoughts of his scrupulous observance of the laws of avoiding forbidden speech.

Yitzchak Heller: Further taking up what Hagi was saying about the connection between theory and practice for Dov, I would like to stress another point that explains this phenomenon – his honesty and integrity. When he dealt with a problem, he dealt with it from every angle. Even when his emotions leaned in a particular direction, he succeeded in analyzing the matter intellectually, dispassionately, although he certainly had a warm heart as well. It had to do with the honesty and integrity that were ingrained in him.

Because of that honesty he never stopped analyzing and criticizing himself, and during those last years he had a lot of doubts. There were long periods when he was dissatisfied with himself. He had the feeling that he wasn't doing enough, that he wasn't making the best use of his time, that he wasn't succeeding as much as he could have and as much as he wanted to. Often, he would examine whether he had to take one path or another.

Ingrained in my memory is a sentence Dov said on the last Erev Yom Kippur [the day before Yom Kippur] of his life. We were sitting in our room several hours before the fast began, and there was a heavy feeling of self-criticism, and then I heard Dov say, "Why must we go on like this? We've wasted another year!" When he examined the year, he concluded that he could have done much more, he could have accomplished much more, he could have exacted from himself much more. It's a shocking sentence, especially on the background of the fact that two days later he fell in battle, sanctifying God's Name.

That same honesty led to his being one in word and deed. When he came to a conclusion, he strove to realize it. An example of this is his having chosen the *hesder* army-plus-Torah-learning program. He wanted to take part in the practical side of the redemption, to carry it out personally. His scrutiny in mitzva observance was linked to this as well. I remember a talk I had with Dov's mother during his last Pesach, when he was in Ras Sudr. She told me that he wasn't eating anything. Because he was being strict with himself about *kashrut*, he ate very little all through Pesach. Interpersonal relations were something else that didn't remain theoretical for Dov. His helpfulness has already been mentioned, as well as his connecting specifically with weaker individuals.

Yitzchak Halperin: I'd like to tell a little story that shows Dov's relationship to forbidden speech. One Rosh Hashana at Netiv Meir, we came across a book by Rabbi Yisrael Meir HaKohen, the Chafetz Chaim, about the laws of forbidden speech, and Dov decided that that Rosh Hashana he would learn the entire work from start to finish. We finished services that night and everyone went to sleep. Dov took up the book and started to learn it, and at the end of the holiday he said, "I finished the book."

Simha: Yitzchak's story gives me an opportunity to stress a point that hasn't been emphasized until now: Dov's academic perseverance. Despite his possessing above-average talents, he didn't rely on those talents, but rather built his success on perseverance. A person can be enormously talented and he can waste those talents entirely. Dov knew that he had to work hard to realize his potential.

Yitzchak Heller: I'd like to go back to a point that Haim spoke about – Dov's openness and worldliness. It was common to see Dov come back from the nighttime study session at eleven or twelve at night, then get into bed but not go to sleep. Sometimes two or three hours would pass from the moment he climbed into bed until he fell asleep. During that time he would deal with a broad range of issues. Sometimes he would solve mathematical problems. Other times he would learn the philosophical writings of Maharal.[4] There was a period when he was reading Agnon a lot.

Hagi: I am presently editing Dov's writings for publication. Whoever reads his writings will encounter quotations from Maharal and from the Chazon Ish, together with quotations and examples out of the books of Viktor Frankl, Eli Wiesel, Sartre, Agnon, *Molière*, and many others.

Yitzchak: And another thing: With Dov, it wasn't just about the study of books, but about the study of people. The people he met – even the simplest person, someone you might think there'd be nothing to learn from – Dov would learn from. He would reach out to him, try to get inside his world and draw out of him whatever it was possible to draw out. During his military service, he tried to get to know secular people as well, and with one such person, Eitan Steif of Ramat Yohanan, he continued to correspond afterwards. This longing to gain familiarity and knowledge about everything found expression in something else as well: Dov, so deep and pensive, loved to go on hikes, and often went on hikes during his vacations. I, personally, went on several hikes with him.

Hagi: I suggest that we pause for a moment in our sketching of Dov's personality and move over a bit to the realm of short stories about Dov.

Simha: Dov would drag a lot of books with him to the army. One Shabbat during basic training, I had to go down to the Suez Canal. This was the first time in my life that I was driving on Shabbat, and it made me kind of sad. Dov noticed this, and he gave me the book *Sefer Mitzvot HaKatan*, which he had with

---

[4] Maharal, Rabbi Yehuda Loew, was a prominent sixteenth-century Talmudic scholar who served as the leading rabbi in the city of Prague. He is known for his works on Jewish philosophy, Jewish mysticism, and his *Gur Aryeh al HaTorah*, a supercommentary on Rashi's Torah commentary.

him in a pocket edition, and he said: "Learn some laws about the Shabbat out of this book and you'll forget that you're traveling by car."

Haim: Shabbat in the army reminds me of something that happened when we were at Ras Sudr. Once on Friday night, I had to do guard duty from nine o'clock till midnight, and Dov had to guard after me from midnight to three o'clock in the morning. We finished the evening service and meal, and I went out to guard. After fifteen minutes Dov came up to my post, sat down, and starting chatting with me. At first I thought that after several minutes he would go down to sleep, but he showed no signs of intending to go to bed. After ten o'clock, I yelled at him that he should go to sleep, so he'd be able to get up for his midnight guard duty. His answer surprised me: "I know you don't like to guard alone, and right now I'm not so tired." Only someone who was a soldier and knows how soldiers try to grab every moment of shut-eye that they can will understand the significance of Dov's behavior.

Reuven: Haim mentioned the Ras Sudr period. That reminds me of a short but very characteristic story about Dov. One night the telephone rang by the yeshiva study hall (I was in yeshiva then). I picked up the receiver and it was Dov calling from Ras Sudr. After the normal questions, like "What's new in yeshiva?" etc., he asked me to give him a summary of the day's Torah lecture by Rabbi Moshe Dimentman. That day there had been a particularly good lecture, and over the phone I repeated for him the content of the lesson. For me, that was an intense experience I will not forget.

Haim: I want to tell you what happened from the other side of the line. When we were at Ras Sudr, the two of us were sent for a week to stand guard at an isolated checkpoint. We were there alone for a whole week, and it was pretty frightening. We had a field telephone there, and at night we would take advantage of its availability to overcome that feeling of being all alone. Dov became friendly over the phone with one of the radio operators, and the fellow would do whatever Dov asked. Every night we'd call another yeshiva. To whichever student answered the phone, we would say that we were religious soldiers and we wanted him to tell us some novel Torah thought that he had learned or had heard during the day. I don't know what those students thought of us, but anyway, they would usually give us interesting Torah insights. We did this every night. The initiator of and active participant in all of these conversations was Dov.

Simha: He had a very serious attitude toward the army, and he viewed military service as a mitzva of the highest importance. He heard from the fellows who had already been in the army that it paid to prepare physically for basic training. He felt he needed a physical head start, and before induction he trained by running almost every night. The guys would sometimes laugh at him, but he wouldn't answer them. I saw that he had written down somewhere, "Be among those insulted; and not among the insulters." He knew that the running was something he had to do, and he did it quietly and seriously. Afterwards he had a harsh struggle in the army, a struggle with physical fitness. I recall that Dov worked very hard. On long hikes he would grit his teeth and repeat to himself, "Don't break! Keep going until the end!" If someone wanted to talk to him, he wouldn't answer, for fear that it would weaken his walking.

Another interesting point: In basic training we were in adjacent beds in our tent. If he had a free moment, he would grab the chance to clean his gun, put his load-bearing equipment in order, and all without any connection to muster or to any other kind of review. Sometimes he would empty his kit bag and reorganize it, without any connection to going home. Just for the heck of it, so that everything would be in tip-top shape. Because of that, I called him Soap.

Conversely, he would get irritated with me over my apathy. He was always rebuking me over my not making enough of an effort in terms of spit and polish, and his words would always include the sentence "If you're in the army, you've got to go all the way with it." It's interesting. Even his rebuke wasn't expressed as a harangue but in a very friendly tone.

Yitzchak Heller: Simha mentioned Dov's great willpower. That's an interesting point. Whenever he was faced with a challenge, it would awaken in him a fierce desire to meet the challenge. He had a tendency to daydream, and often he wasn't on top of what was happening in our Torah lectures. Yet when a challenge was presented, some provocative question, he would turn sharp and alert. It was the same in the army. He set challenges for himself, and to a large extent that's how he kept up. One time in basic training there was a difficult hike involving carrying fellow soldiers on stretchers, and he suffered greatly. As he walked along, holding a stretcher, he would see some light pole in the distance and would resolve that he wasn't going to break until he reached that pole. He would continue until that point, and only then would he ask to be replaced.

Yitzchak Halperin: From all the things said here, and all the stories told here, one could get the feeling that we're talking about some figure who was wonderful but distant, not of this world. I would like to stress that Dov knew how to lead a normal life: to be happy, to sing, to act silly, to lead a really normal life together with everyone else. He wasn't cut off from everyone. Besides thinking, philosophizing, and expressing uncertainties, he also knew how to live like everyone else, and perhaps even better.

Simha: The interesting thing is that not only we, who lived with him, but also his teachers and educators noticed his unique personality. Already in elementary school, he was especially beloved by his teacher, Yaakov Vonderwalde, who wasn't able to hide his affection for Dov, arousing the jealousy of the rest of the students. Also at Netiv Meir, Dov was the teachers' favorite.

At Kerem B'Yavneh, an extraordinary connection was forged between him and the head of the yeshiva, Rabbi Goldvicht. In general, direct contact between Rabbi Goldvicht and students in their first years was limited, but Rabbi Goldvicht already knew Dov the first year, and loved to give him an occasional pat on the shoulder and to exchange a few words with him.

Haim: I'd like to elaborate on a point Yitzchak Halperin touched on – happiness. Anyone who thinks deep thoughts, who isn't shallow, will face uncertainties. Dov, as well, had a lot of uncertainties, especially at crossroads: at the end of yeshiva high school, toward the end of *hesder*. Despite it all, he was always happy. It wasn't the happiness of frivolity, of fooling around, but the happiness of a magnificent soul, of great faith. If you look over his picture albums, you'll almost always find that smile. Even the night after Yom Kippur, when the war broke out and I came to his house, I was surprised to find him smiling. "A war that breaks out on Yom Kippur, when all of Israel is pure, has to end in our victory," he said to explain the happiness that had taken hold of him. This was happiness that emerged from reflection, deep happiness.

Hagi: I remember that night after Yom Kippur as one big nightmare, a frightening hodgepodge. Yet amidst the great chaos, I remember one thing well – that Dov disappeared on me without my even having a chance to say goodbye. I was Dov's guest in yeshiva that Yom Kippur. At the end of Yom Kippur, when we found out what had happened, Dov ran to his room to get some phone tokens so he could call home. I ran after him, but he was already gone. I went back to the telephone, but there they told me that he had already left for Jerusalem. He literally ran to the war like a person running to some good deed he's afraid of missing out on. I remember a sentence I saw in one of Dov's letters: "Life with an ideal worth dying for is a life worth living." Within that sentence is an enormous readiness for self-sacrifice, based on a sense that self-sacrifice is what gives life its flavor, that it is life's essence. It's amazing how connected thought and action were for Dov.

Reuven: I'd like to conclude with several general remarks. One of the problems of youth who grow up in yeshivot is that they lack role models on a high level with whom they can totally identify. Rabbi Abraham Isaac Kook is a central figure in the consciousness of the Bnei Akiva yeshivot, but he is not a living personality who is present among us. The new world of yeshivot is relatively young; hence, it hasn't yet had time to produce well-rounded role models who can serve as a symbol for yeshiva youths.

Under the circumstances, even young people can, to a certain extent, fill the gap. There are young people who have achieved a certain maturity and perfection, and they can provide an example and be a symbol for these youths. I think Dov belongs to this group. Dov can serve as a symbol on several planes. At Kerem B'Yavneh there is a brochure presenting Rabbi Goldvicht's vision for the yeshiva. He writes that it is his ambition to create a blending of the old yeshiva world with the new spirit being forged here in Israel. He does not want to create something cut off from the past, but an integration of two worlds.

Today, in Israel, we find yeshiva youths of the old type, and we also find pioneering youths of the new type. But to find a youth that integrates the two worlds is a bit hard. Dov was among those few whom you could integrate nicely into both the old-world yeshiva of Kfar Hasidim and the new type that Rabbi Goldvicht envisioned for Kerem B'Yavneh. (At the end of high school, Dov thought about continuing on to Kfar Hasidim, and he visited there.)

Dov can serve as a symbol from another perspective as well, which Hagi touched on at the beginning of the evening. The separation between the intellectual side and the ethical side is, unfortunately, rather common in yeshivot. There are learned types and there are righteous types. The accepted standard is that the learned type is arrogant, mocks others, and it's not so easy to become his friend. On the other hand, the various righteous types, those who work all day on the moral treatise *Mesillat Yesharim*, are guys who don't always like the complexities of detailed Talmudic learning. Dov was a prime example of a person who was both profound in his learning and a paragon of kindness and moral rectitude.

Haim: Dov can serve as a symbol in terms of his worldliness as well. A generation of Torah-true Jews of a new stripe has to be, first of all, open: open to different types of people, to different types of voices, to different types of professions. They should have an open mind and an open heart. They should be ready to think one way and to think the other way as well, to listen to one view and to listen to someone else as well. Dov was like that. He had an open mind to learn everything, and an open soul to hear different opinions and different approaches. That's what made him a fascinating conversationalist, and it was possible to spend half a night of guard duty with him without feeling the time passing.

Hagi: The time has come to wind up, and we haven't finished saying everything, and there's the feeling that it was only a beginning. But a clock has its own ideas. I'd like to conclude with a quotation from one of Dov's letters, a paragraph in which Dov speaks of the life of the believer, but he's actually talking about himself, about his own life. It's a sort of concise overview in which a person sums up his own life without knowing it. He writes:

> Seemingly, the life of the believer, who makes use of the "opium of the masses," is easier, since he has no doubts and problems. Yet that isn't really true, since having complete faith imposes on a person not only numerous limitations and prohibitions (which are the easy part), but a relentless effort to transcend the physical and the banal. A believer's life is supposed to be full of crises:

endless ups and downs in his spiritual odyssey, doubts about his ability to keep up in his struggle against the evil impulse, uncertainties, and doubts at crossroads in the pathways of life.

Yet the believer's contentment knows no bounds. It's a contentment that does not derive from wealth or honor, but a pure spiritual contentment that fills the believer with infinite bliss, a bliss that is along the lines of the heavenly reward promised to the righteous. Faith is an ideal that is never ending. "Man is born for toil" (Job 5:7), which our sages interpret to mean "to toil over the Torah." Maharal explains this: "Man is born for a type of toil that can never end, and however much it is brought to fruition, there always remains a potential for more" (*Tiferet Yisrael*, chapter 3).

Headstone of Dov's grave in Givat Shaul גוש ז, חלקה י"ד. *At the request of his father, he was buried next to his grandfather, Arieh Indig, and his grandmother, Chaya Indig. Twenty years after Dov was killed, his father, Avraham Yehezkel Indig, z"tzl passed away.*